THE OFFICIAL 2014
HAMMERS

WEST HAM UNITED

Written by Rob Mason
A TWOCAN PUBLICATION
©2014. Published by twocan under licence
from West Ham United FC.
ISBN 978-1-909872-30-1

YEARBOOK

CONTENTS

AUGUST

Saturday	16	Tottenham Hotspur	H	
Saturday	23	Crystal Palace	A	
Tuesday	26	Sheffield United	H	Capital One Cup 2
Saturday	30	Southampton	H	

SEPTEMBER

Monday	15	Hull City	A	
Saturday	20	Liverpool	H	
Saturday	27	Manchester United	A	

OCTOBER

Sunday	5	Queens Park Rangers	H	
Saturday	18	Burnley	A	
Saturday	25	Manchester City	H	

NOVEMBER

Saturday	1	Stoke City	A	
Saturday	8	Aston Villa	H	
Saturday	22	Everton	A	
Saturday	29	Newcastle United	H	

DECEMBER

Tuesday	2	West Bromwich Albion	A	
Sunday	7	Swansea City	H	
Saturday	13	Sunderland	A	
Saturday	20	Leicester City	H	
Friday	26	Chelsea	A	
Sunday	28	Arsenal	H	

JANUARY

Thursday	1	West Bromwich Albion	H	
Saturday	3			FA Cup Round 3
Saturday	10	Swansea City	A	
Saturday	17	Hull City	H	
Saturday	24			FA Cup Round 4
Saturday	31	Liverpool	A	

FEBRUARY

Saturday	7	Manchester United	H	
Tuesday	10	Southampton	A	
Saturday	14			FA Cup Round 5
Saturday	21	Tottenham Hotspur	A	
Saturday	28	Crystal Palace	H	

MARCH

Tuesday	3	Chelsea	H	
Saturday	7			FA Cup Round 6
Saturday	14	Arsenal	A	
Saturday	21	Sunderland	H	

APRIL

Saturday	4	Leicester City	A	
Saturday	11	Stoke City	H	
Saturday	18	Manchester City	A	FA Cup Semi-Final
Saturday	25	Queens Park Rangers	A	

MAY

Saturday	2	Burnley	H	
Saturday	9	Aston Villa	fA	
Saturday	16	Everton	H	
Sunday	24	Newcastle United	A	
Saturday	30			FA Cup Final

BARCLAYS PREMIER LEAGUE

2014/15

SQUAD NO: 2

POSITION: Defender

DoB: 3 July 1988

SIGNED FROM: FC Midtjylland

PREVIOUS CLUBS: SUB Sonderborg

INTERNATIONAL: New Zealand
(and Denmark up to U21)

SQUAD NO: 3

POSITION: Defender

DoB: 15 December 1989

SIGNED FROM: Ipswich Town

PREVIOUS CLUBS: Tranmere Rovers

THE SQUAD 2014/15

WINSTON **REID**

Born in New Zealand of Maori heritage, Winston moved to Denmark when he was ten and went on to represent Denmark up to U21 level before deciding to play for his country of birth.

He made his debut for New Zealand in May 2010 against Australia and that summer Winston started all three of New Zealand's games at the FIFA World Cup in South Africa. He scored a last minute equaliser against Slovakia and after further draws with Italy and Paraguay his team emerged as the tournament's only unbeaten country.

The positive impression Winston created at the FIFA World Cup led to him joining the Hammers in August of that year, debuting at Aston Villa ten days after his arrival. A dozen games in all competitions in his first season established Reid as a regular in his second season when he appeared 33 times. His best season so far came in 2012/13 when he missed just two Barclays Premier League games and was named Hammer of the Year.

Unfortunately, an ankle injury cost him three months in the middle of last season, a spell that coincided in him missing New Zealand's crucial FIFA World Cup Inter-Continental play-off with Mexico.

AARON **CRESSWELL**

A summer 2014 purchase for an undisclosed fee from Ipswich Town, his form with the Blues had seen him named in the PFA Championship team of the Year for 2013/14.

The Liverpool-born full-back began his career with Tranmere Rovers, making his Football League debut in November 2008 in a 1-0 defeat at MK Dons.

Three seasons at Prenton Park saw over half of his 76 appearances come in his final campaign before a move to Ipswich Town in the summer of 2011. Aaron immediately excelled, becoming the Tractor Boys' Player of the Year in his first season.

Having secured him on a five-year deal, the Hammers will see the best years of Cresswell's career, which will hopefully continue on an upward curve.

KEVIN NOLAN

Kevin's consistency means he has made at least 30 League appearances in each of the last 14 seasons, but a shoulder injury suffered early this season kept him out of action for five weeks.

He is so important to West Ham that his return after injury, as a sub in the late-September game at Manchester United, was a massive boost to the squad. With his will to win allied with his ability to score from an attacking midfield position, Kevin is a talisman for the side. He has scored 30 goals in his three full seasons at the Boleyn Ground, being top scorer last season with seven goals.

He was a promotion winner with West Ham, captaining them in the 2012 Play-Off Final win over Blackpool at Wembley, just two years after skippering Newcastle United to the Championship title, and eleven years after winning promotion with his first club Bolton Wanderers.

He joined Bolton as a 16-year-old and went on to become club captain and a key player for them in the best spell of the Trotters' modern history.

After 345 games for Bolton, during which he scored half a century worth of goals, Kevin moved to Newcastle United for £4m in January 2009 and became Championship Player of the Year in his first full season on Tyneside. At West Ham Nolan was named Player of the Month for three months running in the autumn of 2012.

JAMES TOMKINS

Connected to West Ham since first attracting the Club's attention as a seven-year-old, James has been schooled in the West Ham way, with just an eight game stint on loan to Derby County in 2009 breaking his time in Claret and Blue.

James made his breakthrough at the Boleyn Ground when debuting for the first team in March 2008. Gradually building up his first team involvement, Tomkins' time really arrived in 2011/12 when he played a total of 47 times and earned a place in the Championship Team of the Season, as well as being named runner-up in the Hammer of the Year.

That form helped James gain a place in Team GB at the 2012 Olympics where he played against the UAE. Internationally, James has also represented England at every level from U16 to U21, first representing the Three Lions in 2004 and playing in two U21 European Championships.

He began this season just a few games short of 200 for the Hammers and as a 25-year-old has every chance to go on to amass many more appearances.

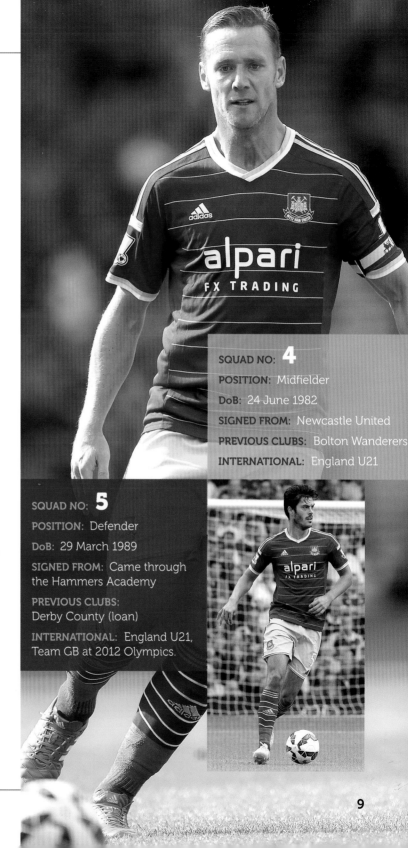

SQUAD NO: **4**
POSITION: Midfielder
DoB: 24 June 1982
SIGNED FROM: Newcastle United
PREVIOUS CLUBS: Bolton Wanderers
INTERNATIONAL: England U21

SQUAD NO: **5**
POSITION: Defender
DoB: 29 March 1989
SIGNED FROM: Came through the Hammers Academy
PREVIOUS CLUBS: Derby County (loan)
INTERNATIONAL: England U21, Team GB at 2012 Olympics.

MATT JARVIS

Millwall released the Middlesbrough-born winger as a 16-year-old, but Matt has bounced back to reach the Barclays Premier League and represent England. Resurrecting his career with Gillingham, Jarvis stepped out for his senior debut as a substitute in a home Championship defeat at the hands of Sunderland in November 2003.

Matt made his name with the Gills, topping a century of games for them and earning a move to Molineux when Wolverhampton Wanderers signed him in June 2007, after he had been included in the League One Team of the Year. After helping Wolves to win promotion to the Barclays Premier League, Jarvis made his bow in the top flight against West Ham in August 2009.

2010/11 was a great season for Matt. He not only played for England at Wembley against Ghana but also won both the Players' Player and Supporters' Player of the Season awards.

A year later West Ham made Jarvis a then-Club record signing, capturing his signature in August 2012 on a five-year deal. Matt made 34 appearances in his first season for the Hammers and played 35 games last term.

CHEIKHOU KOUYATE

This powerful 6'4" central midfielder arrived at the Boleyn Ground in June 2014. He joined for an undisclosed fee from Anderlecht with whom he had won four Belgian League titles and gained extensive Champions League and Europa League experience.

A graduate of the FC Brussels academy, Kouyate had come to Belgium as a 17-year-old and made such an impression that after just ten league games the country's top club Anderlecht swooped to sign him in 2008.

With his first club in Senegal, Cheikhou helped ASC Yego Dakar win the League title and reach the final of the Senegal Junior Cup. In 2012, he took part in the Olympic Games and has also reached double figures in international appearances for Senegal. Kouyate made his debut for the Hammers on the opening day of this season against Tottenham Hotspur.

ANDY CARROLL

An ankle injury sustained in the build-up to the 2014/15 season is expected to delay Andy's return to action until shortly before Christmas. Injury has blighted Carroll's career since joining West Ham which is frustrating as when he is fit, Andy is a powerful weapon and was good enough to win the Chairman's Player of the Year award in 2012/13.

West Ham have long been aware of the danger Carroll poses since marking his full home debut for Newcastle with a powerful header against the Hammers in January 2009. He actually first appeared for the Magpies as a 17-year-old sub in a 2006 UEFA Cup tie against Palermo.

In the intervening period he spent six months on loan at Preston North End, scoring his first goal in November 2007 against Leicester City. That Championship experience proved useful as following Newcastle's relegation Andy became their top scorer with 19 goals in all competitions as they won promotion. He then made it into the 2009/10 Championship Team of the Year.

By now a fearsome presence, especially in the air, he plundered eleven goals in 19 games in the top flight including a hat-trick against Aston Villa. This persuaded Liverpool to make him history's most expensive English player when investing £35m on the final day of the January 2011 transfer window. Nine goals came Andy's way in his first full season at Anfield, including a Wembley winner against Everton in the FA Cup semi-final. He would go on to score in the final too after coming on as a sub, but couldn't stop his side losing to Chelsea as Liverpool sought to secure a domestic cup double with Andy having already helped the Merseysiders beat Cardiff City in the League Cup Final.

Wembley seemed to be becoming Andy's second home at this time, his first goal for England coming in March 2011 against Ghana, four months after his full international debut.

He went on to play and score for England at Euro 2012 and joined West Ham, initially on loan at the end of August 2012. Going into this season Carroll had claimed nine goals in 40 appearances for the Club.

SQUAD NO: 9

POSITION: Centre forward

DoB: 6 January 1989

SIGNED FROM: Liverpool

PREVIOUS CLUBS: Newcastle United, Preston North End (loan).

INTERNATIONAL: England

11

MAURO ZARATE

A skilful and dynamic forward capable of the spectacular, Zarate came into senior football shortly after his 17th birthday when debuting for Velez Sarsfield in his native Argentina in April 2004.

Used extensively as an impact sub in the early years of his career - winning the Primera Division Clausura title in 2005 - Mauro became a regular in 2007, a year when his performances at the FIFA U20 World Cup underlined his ability, not least through his winning goal in the final against the Czech Republic.

The summer of 2007 brought a lucrative move to Al Sadd in Qatar where he scored four times in a dozen games before a January 2008 move to Birmingham City at a time when David Sullivan, David Gold and Karren Brady were in charge at St Andrews. Making his debut at Sunderland, he hit a purple patch after a couple of months with four goals in as many games including two in a win over Manchester City.

He was to net another brace on his debut for Lazio against Cagliari having moved to the Serie A outfit in the summer of 2008. While Lazio were Zarate's third club in a year, he was to settle in Rome, spending three seasons at the Stadio Olimpico before a year in Milan on loan to Internazionale (scoring in a Champions League away win at CSKA Moscow). He spent a further year with Lazio prior to a return to his first club Velez Sarsfield in Argentina in July 2013. He was to win the Argentina Supercopa, Zarate playing in the final against Arsenal de Sarandi - the club he'd debuted against almost a decade earlier.

Now 27 he has decided to have another crack at the Barclays Premier League having been persuaded to sign for West Ham on a three-year contract. He made an immediate impression with a debut goal in a comprehensive 3-1 win at Crystal Palace in August.

SQUAD NO: **10**

POSITION: Forward

DoB: 18 March 1987

SIGNED FROM: Velez Sarsfield

PREVIOUS CLUBS: Al Sadd (Qatar) Birmingham City, Lazio, Internazionale (loan),

INTERNATIONAL: Argentina U20

STEWART DOWNING

An experienced England international winger who moved to West Ham on a four-year contract in August 2013, Stewart ended his first season at West Ham with a goal against Spurs and began his second campaign with another strike, this time against Crystal Palace.

Whilst at Liverpool he scored in the penalty shoot-out as they won the Carling Cup in 2012, a trophy he had won eight years earlier with Middlesbrough as an unused sub in the final. Two years later Stewart was in 'Boro's starting line up for the UEFA Cup Final as they lost to Seville.

In between his spells with 'Boro and Liverpool, Downing played for Aston Villa where he was Player of the Year in 2010/11. He has also won seasonal individual awards at his other two permanent clubs.

After a handful of League starts in his first three years with his home-town club on Teesside, Downing excelled on loan at Sunderland, being recalled after three goals in seven games. From there, Stewart went from strength to strength, soon making his full England debut at his future home ground of Villa Park in 2004.

Two years later, Downing came off the bench three times at the 2006 FIFA World Cup in Germany. Although he did not appear in the finals, Stewart was selected by England for their Euro 2012 campaign.

RICARDO VAZ TE

The scorer of the 87th minute winner in the 2012 Championship Play-Off Final against Blackpool, Ricardo had scored a hat-trick a month earlier, with one of those goals against Brighton - a spectacular scissor kick - winning the Club's Goal of the Season award.

Taking home the match ball that night, Vaz Te could reflect on having scored eight goals in his last five games, notching in all of them, including one against former club Barnsley. Now that's what you call a purple patch - but the best was to come at Wembley.

Ricardo had come to the club in the January transfer window, manager Sam Allardyce having brought him to the Boleyn Ground from Barnsley. Big Sam previously nurtured Vaz Te, having brought him into English football when signing him for Bolton in 2003.

Born in Lisbon, Ricardo had spent much of his childhood in Guinea-Bissau in West Africa prior to a return to Portugal where he developed his game before coming into English football as a 17-year-old.

He remained with Bolton for six seasons, with a brief loan at Hull along the way, but moved into Greek football in 2010/11, returning to Britain north of the border with Hibernian later the same season before a goal laden spell at Barnsley. As a Tyke he averaged a goal every two games despite almost half his appearances being off the bench. His dozen strikes included a hat-trick in a derby win over Leeds, a feat that ended a run of eight goals in as many games, strikingly similar to his purple patch in Claret and Blue!

SQUAD NO: **11**

POSITION: Winger

DoB: 22 July 1984

SIGNED FROM: Liverpool

PREVIOUS CLUBS: Middlesbrough, Sunderland (loan), Aston Villa

INTERNATIONAL: England

SQUAD NO: **12**

POSITION: Forward

DoB: 1 October 1986

SIGNED FROM: Barnsley

PREVIOUS CLUBS: Real Massama, SC Farense, Bolton Wanderers, Hull City (loan), Panionios, Hibs

INTERNATIONAL: Portugal U21

ADRIAN

Real Betis suffered relegation the season after Adrian left them to come to West Ham. In his season as their first choice 'keeper - 2012/13 - he kept clean sheets in a third of his appearances - eleven in 31 - as Betis achieved a healthy seventh place.

Adrian's performances attracted rave reviews, none more so than a Man-of-the-Match display as Real Madrid were beaten 1-0 in November 2012. Adrian San Miguel del Castillo, to give him his full name, evidently likes a challenge. In his first season at the Boleyn Ground last year he scooped the award for Best Individual Performance for his display at Chelsea, doubling up with the Best Save award for a save in the same game when he denied Oscar.

Although he had made several cup appearances, Adrian had to wait until the Saturday before Christmas for his first opportunity in the Barclays Premier League. When it came, he grabbed his opportunity with both hands, winning the Player of the Month award in both January and February. He continued to do so well that by the end of the campaign, he was named as the Signing of the Season, going on to begin the current campaign as first choice goalkeeper despite competition from Jussi Jaaskelainen.

Born in Seville, Adrian was with local side Betis from the age of ten, making his way through lower league football in his homeland both through loans and Betis' B and C teams who operate lower down the footballing tiers in Spain.

SQUAD NO: **13**

POSITION: Goalkeeper

DoB: 3 January 1987

SIGNED FROM: Real Betis

PREVIOUS CLUBS: SD Alcala (loan), CD Utera (loan) plus Real Betis B & Real Betis C

RAVEL **MORRISON**

Never was Ravel Morrison's potential better illustrated than with his sublime goal in the handsome 3-0 win at Tottenham Hotspur in October 2013. Ravel has wonderful skill and his challenge is to channel it into the team pattern and look to make maximum use of his ability on a consistent basis.

Morrison can be a match-winner. His balance, vision and skill are vital ingredients providing he can find the recipe for success. Manchester-born, Ravel came through the Manchester United youth system debuting as a 17-year-old in the League Cup in October 2010 and going on to appear twice in the same competition the following season before being allowed to sign for West Ham in January 2012, when still in his teens.

Given a debut at Leeds two months after signing, he was subsequently allowed to go on loan to Birmingham City in 2012/13. He became a key player at St Andrews, playing 30 times, all but four of them being starts. Returning to West Ham last season he began well, scoring his first Hammers goal in the Capital One Cup against Cheltenham, three days after appearing in the Barclays Premier League at Newcastle. His first top flight goal arrived three weeks later with another cup goal coming just three days after that.

The goals and performances kept coming, that brilliant effort at Spurs being followed up with another strike at Norwich the following month. In February he was loaned out to QPR helping the Hoops to promotion. Morrison once again showed his worth and he began this season back in the Hammers starting line up for the Capital One Cup tie with Sheffield United, before being loaned out to Cardiff City.

DIAFRA **SAKHO**

It is hardly surprising that Diafra Sakho is quick. He only began playing football seriously as a 17-year-old having concentrated on running 100m and 200m before that.

Sakho quickly moved up-front from his original central midfield position. Diafra became a hero with Metz in France where 50 goals in 126 games included a terrific haul of 43 in the last two seasons as he fired Metz from the third tier in France - the Championnat National - to the top flight.

Last year he was named as the Ligue 2 Player of the Year as Metz strode to the title on the back of Sakho's 20 goals in 36 games. Such form propelled Diafra into his national team, his first two appearances arriving in May 2014, scoring in the second of them. An undisclosed fee brought him across the Channel to West Ham on a four-year deal two days before the start of the season. Given the final 20 minutes on the second weekend of the season at Crystal Palace, Sakho then marked his home debut, and first start, with a well-taken header in the Capital One Cup meeting with Sheffield United.

SQUAD NO: **14**

POSITION: Midfielder

DoB: 2 February 1993

SIGNED FROM: Manchester Utd

PREVIOUS CLUBS: Birmingham City (loan), QPR (loan)

INTERNATIONAL: England U21

SQUAD NO: **15**

POSITION: Striker

DoB: 24 December 1989

SIGNED FROM: Metz

PREVIOUS CLUBS: Medina, Boulogne (loan)

INTERNATIONAL: Senegal

SQUAD NO: **16**

POSITION: Midfielder DoB: 8 May 1987
SIGNED FROM: Came through the Hammers Academy
PREVIOUS CLUBS: Hull City (loan), Ipswich Town (loan)
INTERNATIONAL: England U21

MARK **NOBLE**

Mark is West Ham's longest serving player and current Hammer of the Year and Players' Player of the Year. He started this season 12 games short of 300 appearances for the Club at the age of 27. Mark's appearance at Crystal Palace as captain at the start of this season came a day before the tenth anniversary of his first team debut.

Over the last decade the man from Canning Town has lived through all of the Club's ups and downs. He has been at the heart of the good times and never gone missing in the dark days.

Mark's teenage years saw him gradually nudge himself into the team. 13 starts and eight substitute appearances in his first season included appearing in the Play-Off Final win over Preston North End at the Millennium Stadium. The step up to the top flight saw his appearances reduced, leading to him going on loan to Hull City in February 2006 to broaden his experience. The following season he added to that by going on a hugely successful loan to Ipswich, playing 13 times (in addition to the five games he had played for Hull). Returning to the Boleyn Ground in mid-November he went on to reach double figures in West Ham League appearances, notching a couple of goals along the way as his all-action attitude endeared him to fans and team-mates alike.

From then on Noble became more and more a regular in the Hammers' side - 2009/10 when he appeared 28 times being the only subsequent season when he has not played in at least 30 matches. Indeed he was ever-present in the League last season and missed just one League or Play-Off game out of 49 in 2011/12 when he was Hammer of the Year for the first time. That campaign also saw Mark take the Individual Performance of the Season award for his display against Nottingham Forest, which took the Hammers to the top of the table after he scored two of his trademark penalties.

A terrific ambassador for the Club, Mark Noble represents all that is good about West Ham United.

JOEY **O'BRIEN**

Joey's eleventh appearance of this season will mark his 100th for the Hammers who he joined on a free transfer in July 2011. Like Ricardo Vaz Te, O'Brien was given an opportunity to come to West Ham having previously played for Sam Allardyce at Bolton.

O'Brien had played just 13 games in three seasons when he was taken on. A long fight against knee injuries, which had seen him not play at all in 2009/10, ultimately proved successful as Joey's determination to focus on his rehabilitation and return to playing finally paid off. Indeed that renaissance seemed complete a year after joining West Ham when he was capped by his country after a four-year gap since his previous cap.

That first year at West Ham had seen O'Brien prove his fitness by starting 28 games and making a further five appearances off the bench. A year later he started 32 Barclays Premier League fixtures and while last season he played just 20 times in all competitions he was in the starting line-up for the opening games of this season.

September 2014 marked a decade since Joey's senior debut for Bolton. That came in a League Cup tie after which he gained experience on loan at Sheffield Wednesday, the Owls being a club he would return to in March 2011 as he looked to resurrect his career after injury.

CARL **JENKINSON**

Securing 22-year-old England international Carl Jenkinson on a season-long loan from Arsenal is a quality addition to the Irons' squad. Unfortunately, three days after joining the Club, Jenkinson sustained a hamstring injury after an hour of his first appearance against Malaga in Gelsenkirchen and was subsequently ruled out of the start of the season.

Harlow-born, Carl made his debut as a sub for Charlton in a defeat at Hartlepool the day after Valentine's Day in 2011. He did well enough to earn a start in the next game and keep his place for seven games. A similar pattern had occurred earlier in the season during a loan to Conference side Eastbourne Borough. Four days after Guy Fawkes Night, Jenkinson had debuted as a sub against Forest Green Rovers and impressed enough to earn starts in the following three fixtures.

Ten months after stepping into the Conference ahead of his Football League debut, Carl was playing Champions League football. Arsene Wenger signed him in June 2011 and almost immediately pitched the teenager into a Gunners debut against Udinese. That debut was one of four European games Carl featured in during his first season which also brought nine Premier League outings as well as one in the League Cup.

In each of the last two seasons he has played in 14 Barclays Premier League games with a combined tally of a further eight Champions League appearances plus seven domestic cup games. Progressing at Arsenal, Carl has also made a full international debut for England, playing against Sweden in November 2012. As well as previously representing England at U21 level, Jenkinson had also played three times as an U21 player for Finland, qualifying for them through his mother.

SQUAD NO: **17**

POSITION: Defender

DoB: 17 February 1986

SIGNED FROM: Bolton Wanderers

PREVIOUS CLUBS:
Sheffield Wednesday (loan)

INTERNATIONAL:
Republic of Ireland

SQUAD NO: **18**

POSITION: Defender

DoB: 8 February 1992

SIGNED FROM: Arsenal on a season-long loan

PREVIOUS CLUBS: Charlton Athletic, Eastbourne Borough (loan)

INTERNATIONAL: England (and Finland at junior level)

SQUAD NO: 19

POSITION: Defender

DoB: 23 August 1983

SIGNED FROM: Aston Villa

PREVIOUS CLUBS: Cardiff City

INTERNATIONAL: Wales

SQUAD NO: 20

POSITION: Defender

DoB: 13 June 1981

SIGNED FROM: Hamburger SV

PREVIOUS CLUBS: Nimes Olympique, Arsenal, Borussia Dortmund.

INTERNATIONAL: Ivory Coast

JAMES COLLINS

An experienced Wales international defender now in his second spell with West Ham. Initially at the Boleyn Ground from July 2005 to September 2009 when he amassed 63 appearances, he was just a handful of games short of equalling that tally at the start of this season, although an opening-day red card against Tottenham delayed him being able to overtake that total in this his second spell.

Collins returned to West Ham in August 2012 after three seasons with Aston Villa for whom he played 107 times after costing them a reported £5m fee. Oddly enough James' second debut for West Ham came against none other than Villa. Perhaps inevitably, he walked away with the Man of the Match award having excelled in a Hammers victory. Collins began his career in his native Wales, coming through the junior ranks at Cardiff City. Debuting as a 17-year-old in November 2000 he was given a late taste of action with an FA Cup clash against Bristol Rovers already handsomely tied up.

Quietly nurtured by the Bluebirds over the next few seasons he helped them to promotion to the Championship in 2003 and made his full international debut in May 2004. The following season he became a regular with Cardiff, also being named Welsh Young Player of the Year. That summer West Ham made a double swoop for James and fellow defender Danny Gabbidon, Collins going on to register 18 starts in his first season in London. He continued to develop until a horrendous injury picked up in a reserve game in January 2008 ruled him out for ten months.

GUY DEMEL

As with Carl Jenkinson, Guy Demel found himself signed by Arsenal soon after making a first team breakthrough. Indeed Orsay-born Guy had played just one senior game in his native France for Nimes when Arsene Wenger brought him to London in 2000/01.

It remains the only game Demel has played for a French club and indeed he had to wait over a decade to play for an English club when he debuted for West Ham in November 2011. He never made a first-team appearance for the Gunners and after a solitary season at Arsenal, Demel went on to make his name and enjoy considerable success in Germany. Three seasons on the fringes at Borussia Dortmund were followed by six seasons at Hamburg. Oddly his first game for Dortmund was in France, a Champions League game at Auxerre, while his Bundesliga debut came in March 2003 in a home win over Hansa Rostock. His second Bundesliga appearance being in a notable home victory over Bayern Munich.

Towards the end of his second season in Germany, Guy made his international debut, coming on as a 75th minute substitute for Ivory Coast in a 2-0 World Cup qualifying win over Libya. He would go on to be part of the Ivorians' squad for the 2006 FIFA World Cup in Germany and although he didn't get a game he did go on to start two group games four years later at the FIFA World Cup in South Africa as well as appearing in the 2008 Africa Cup of Nations.

Never able to nail down a regular place at Dortmund, Demel departed for Hamburg in 2005, scoring on his debut in an Intertoto Cup game against Pobeda in July. He would net a more significant goal the following March as he helped Hamburg to beat Bayern Munich. Later the same calendar year he got the chance to play against his former club Arsenal in the Champions League, although Arsene Wenger's men triumphed on that occasion. There was a better experience against a former club in August 2008 though, when Guy scored in a 4-1 thumping of Borussia Dortmund.

After six seasons and close to 200 games for Hamburg, Guy returned to London in August 2011 signing for West Ham and helping the Club to promotion in his first season. Going on to appear in 63 out of 76 Barclays Premier League games in the last two years, Guy's versatility remains an asset as he is able to operate in midfield or central defence as well as at right back.

MORGAN **AMALFITANO**

Signed for an undisclosed fee from Marseille as the summer transfer window drew to a close, Amalfitano has a year's experience of the Barclays Premier League having spent last season on loan to West Bromwich Albion for whom he scored on his home debut against Sunderland in what was Paolo Di Canio's final match in charge of the Black Cats. Amalfitano followed that up with a goal in Albion's win at Manchester United and would go on to add two more strikes in 30 appearances in all competitions for the Baggies.

Scoring goals has always been something of a bonus for Morgan who is more a maker than a taker of goals. Indeed he didn't score at all for his first club Sedan for whom he played over 120 games in four years. His first appearance for Sedan came in August 2004 when he came on for the last 14 minutes of a 3-2 win over Lorient, a club he would join four years later.

Morgan's first season saw him start 19 games and come on as sub a further seven times, including coming off the bench to help Sedan win 1-0 against Monaco in the Coupe de France semi-final in May 2005. He would play in another semi-final for Sedan three years later, this time the full game in a 1-0 defeat at the hands of Lyon. That summer Morgan would move on to Lorient, debuting as a sub in a 1-0 win at Le Mans in August.

His first goal for Lorient came in a 3-2 win at Marseille in November 2008, Amalfitano striking ten minutes after coming off the bench. The second of three seasons with Lorient brought six goals including two in one match against Valenciennes just before Christmas 2009, a season that would bring an appearance in the semi-final of the Coupe de la Ligue, a vintage Bordeaux performance seeing off Morgan's men however.

2011 brought a major move to Marseille for whom Morgan debuted in a 5-4 Trophee des Champions win over Lille. His first season at Marseille would bring nine appearances in the Champions League including games against Bayern Munich, Inter and Arsenal. The same campaign would also bring, what to date is, his only full international appearance, appearing for the final 22 minutes of a Leap Year day win over Germany. Further success would come six weeks later when he played the full game as Marseille beat Lyon in the final of the Coupe de la Ligue, perhaps a touch of revenge for his 2008 semi-final defeat at the hands of Lyon when with Sedan.

SQUAD NO: **21**

POSITION: Midfielder

DoB: 20 March 1985

SIGNED FROM: Marseille

PREVIOUS CLUBS: Sedan, Lorient, West Bromwich Albion (loan)

INTERNATIONAL: France

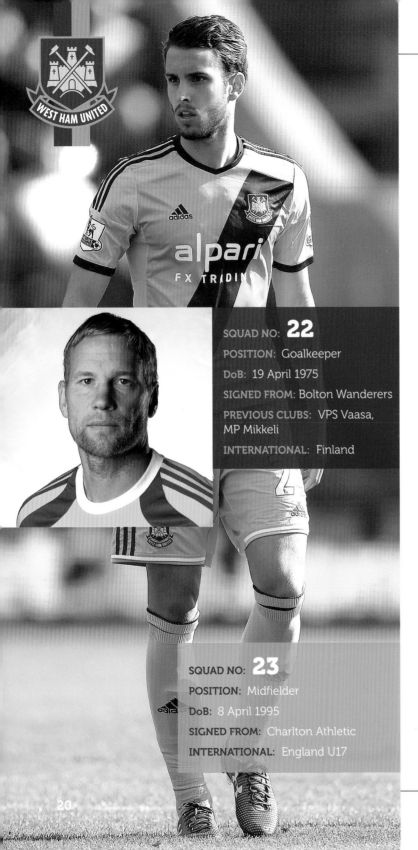

JUSSI **JAASKELAINEN**

One of the most agile and consistent goalkeepers to play in the Premier League era, Jussi is a veteran who will turn 40 before the end of the season. He has been an ever-present in the top flight on seven occasions, the most recent of these was with West Ham in 2012/13, his first season with the Club.

Previously Jaaskelainen had spent 14 seasons with Bolton Wanderers who he joined in 1997 for perhaps the best £100,000 Bolton ever spent in the modern era. Having helped them to promotion in 2001, Jussi helped to establish Sam Allardyce's Trotters as a top-flight outfit good enough to never finish out of the top eight in a four season spell, as well as reach the League Cup Final and play in Europe.

Bolton's Player of the Year in 2007, he was also Finnish Footballer of the Year in the same season. Jussi made 56 appearances for his country between 1998 and 2010.

Moving to the Boleyn Ground in July 2012, Jaaskelainen twice won the Player of the Month award and finished runner-up to Winston Reid as Hammer of the Year. Starting his second season as first choice - as you would expect after being ever-present in the Barclays Premier League - Jussi kept three clean sheets in his opening four games taking his overall tally to 14 in 42 - exactly one for every three appearances.

A regular up to Christmas, he came under pressure from the outstanding form of Adrian and went into this season as his back-up. Jussi appeared early on in the Capital One Cup against Sheffield United and has topped 700 club games in his distinguished career having reached triple figures before leaving his homeland to come to England.

DIEGO **POYET**

Much sought after at international level, Diego has represented England at U16 and U17 level but is eligible for the country of his birth, Spain, or the country of his father, Uruguay. There was similar competition for his signature after his contract ran out at Charlton Athletic where he had just become Player of the Year after making his debut in January.

Having decided his future lay with West Ham, Diego was given an early opportunity, coming off the bench for his Barclays Premier League debut at Crystal Palace before being handed his first start and home debut in the Capital One Cup against Sheffield United, when he converted a penalty in the shoot-out.

The son of Gus Poyet, Diego was born in Zaragoza, his father playing for Real Zaragoza at the time, but he has grown up in England having moved here when his father was transferred to Chelsea when Diego was two.

Having signed a four-year contract with West Ham, Poyet, who will turn 20 shortly before the end of the season, is a very highly rated player who we hope to see the best of.

SQUAD NO: **22**

POSITION: Goalkeeper

DoB: 19 April 1975

SIGNED FROM: Bolton Wanderers

PREVIOUS CLUBS: VPS Vaasa, MP Mikkeli

INTERNATIONAL: Finland

SQUAD NO: **23**

POSITION: Midfielder

DoB: 8 April 1995

SIGNED FROM: Charlton Athletic

INTERNATIONAL: England U17

CARLTON COLE

Carlton came to West Ham in July 2006 after spending the formative years of his career with Chelsea, combined with a trio of loans including season-long stints with Aston Villa and Charlton. A Chelsea debutant in April 2002, appearances for Cole were few and far between despite him notching seven goals from five starts in his first two seasons, when he also appeared 14 times off the bench.

Used mainly as a sub in his initial year at the Boleyn Ground, Carlton became more of a regular in 2007/08 before really hitting the goal trail. Reaching double figures in the Barclays Premier League for two successive seasons, he couldn't prevent West Ham going down in 2011 despite being top scorer with eleven goals in all competitions. Determined to help the Hammers straight back to the top table, Cole contributed 15 goals the following season including one in the successful Play-Off Final as he finished as top scorer in the promotion campaign.

Having returned to the top flight, Carlton found his place under pressure and left the club at the end of the season, only to return in October, going on to notch some notable goals and once again give his all for the cause as he leads the line. He started this season positively with a goal at Palace, his 66th for the club.

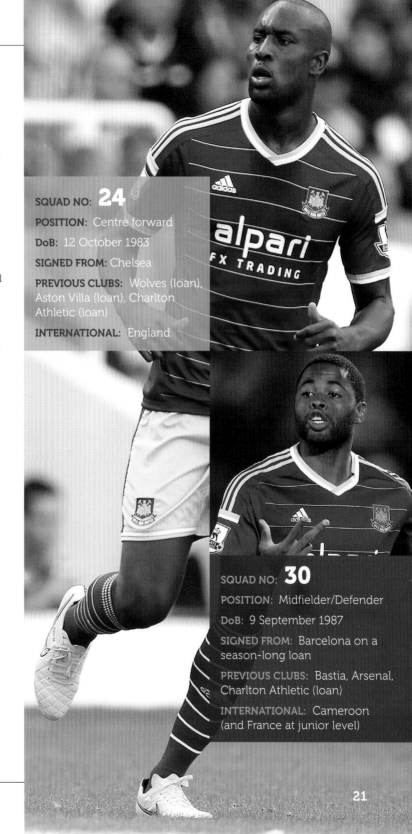

SQUAD NO: **24**

POSITION: Centre forward

DoB: 12 October 1983

SIGNED FROM: Chelsea

PREVIOUS CLUBS: Wolves (loan), Aston Villa (loan), Charlton Athletic (loan)

INTERNATIONAL: England

ALEX SONG

Alex is a top class player on loan from Barcelona, who paid a reported £15m to sign him from Arsenal in August 2012. An established Cameroon international, Alex played in the last two FIFA World Cups and also the 2008 and 2010 Africa Cup of Nations, when he was named in the Team of the Tournament on both occasions, being a finalist in 2008.

Originally with Bastia for whom he played almost 30 games in 2004/05, Alexandre Dimitri Song Billong, to give him his full name, represented France at U16 level before later deciding to play for Cameroon.

He first came to English football when Arsenal acquired him. Initially taking Song on loan in August 2005, the Gunners invested a reported fee of £1m the following June to complete his transfer. Alex's debut had come as a sub against Everton in September 2005 and while that was one of only nine appearances in his year-long loan, Arsene Wenger had seen enough to want to keep Song who was allowed out on loan to Charlton after completing his move.

Over the next few seasons Song became a regular member of the Arsenal side, making 122 Barclays Premier League appearances in the last four of his seven seasons with the club. Hammers fans no doubt will recall a late goal he scored with a diving header against West Ham to give the Gunners a 1-0 victory at the Emirates in October 2010.

Having attracted the interest of Barcelona, Song debuted against Real Madrid and made 20 league appearances in his first season as Barca were crowned Champions in Spain. Last season Alex played one fewer game in La Liga and was an unused sub in the Copa Del Rey Final when Barca lost to Real Madrid.

SQUAD NO: **30**

POSITION: Midfielder/Defender

DoB: 9 September 1987

SIGNED FROM: Barcelona on a season-long loan

PREVIOUS CLUBS: Bastia, Arsenal, Charlton Athletic (loan)

INTERNATIONAL: Cameroon (and France at junior level)

SQUAD NO: **31**

POSITION: Striker

DoB: 4 November 1989

SIGNED FROM: Pachuca

PREVIOUS CLUBS: Club Sport Emelec

INTERNATIONAL: Ecuador

ENNER **VALENCIA**

A star of the 2014 FIFA World Cup where he scored three goals, Ecuador striker Enner Valencia was secured on a five-year contract for an undisclosed fee. Last season he scored 18 goals in 23 Mexican League games as his club finished runners up in the Torneo Clausura.

He had joined Pachuca in January 2014 having starred in his own country where he had helped CS Emelec to win the League title in 2013. It climaxed an exciting four years for Valencia at Emelec. In 2012 they reached the championship finals while in the two previous seasons they had played in the Copa Libertadores. He also gained experience of the Copa Sudamerica where he averaged over a goal a game.

The scorer of seven international goals in 13 appearances prior to his move to West Ham, his debut had come in February 2012 against Honduras. He netted his first international goal against the same opposition 18 months later and bagged two against the Hondurans in Brazil last summer when he also found the net against Switzerland.

Given an early opportunity in England, appearing off the bench on the opening day of the season against Spurs, Enner will look to give the Hammers more firepower up front and showed exactly what he is capable of with an absolutely stunning goal at Hull City in mid-September.

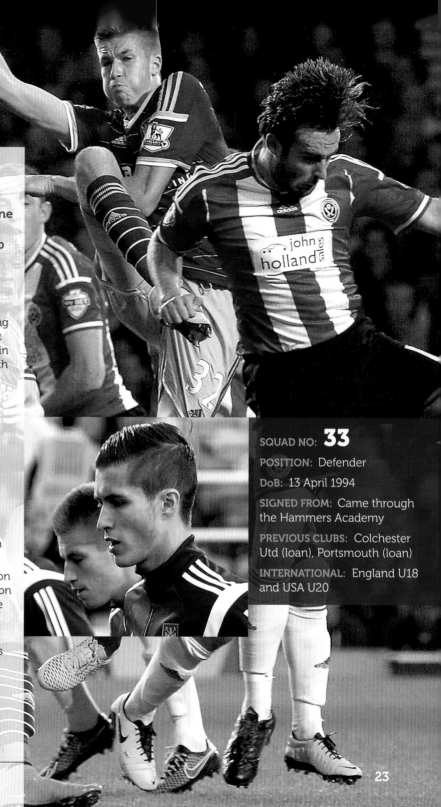

SQUAD NO: 32

POSITION: Defender

DoB: 2 September 1996

SIGNED FROM: Came through the Hammers Academy

REECE BURKE

A teenager who earned a full debut at the start of this season against Sheffield United in the Capital One Cup, Reece had made his first appearance just four months after his 17th birthday when playing as a sub against Nottingham Forest in last season's FA Cup with Budweiser.

Hailing from Hornchurch, Burke has been progressing through the Hammers' Academy since he was nine years old. He made the headlines last summer when scoring the winning goal in the last minute from a move he started and finished at the Boleyn Ground as Italian outfit Sampdoria were defeated in the pre-season Marathonbet Cup. Burke had also travelled with the first-team squad to Germany, playing in the Schalke Cup against Malaga.

DAN POTTS

Like Diego Poyet, Dan has a famous footballing father - Steve Potts having played over 500 times for the Hammers.

Dan made his first team debut against Barnsley in December 2011, a day after signing his first professional contract at the age of seventeen-and-a-half. Not surprisingly he won the Young Hammer of the Year award after making four first team appearances and captaining the youth team that season.

He made eleven senior appearances in 2012/13, five of them on loan to Colchester, and started a game in each cup competition for West Ham last season when he secured further experience with a loan to Portsmouth.

He commenced the current campaign by representing West Ham in the League Cup for the third successive season and as the campaign wears on he will look to earn Barclays Premier League game time as well as Cup experience.

In 2011 he played for the USA at U20 level against France, qualifying through his American-born father but ten months later played at U18 level for the country of his birth, England, in a win over Poland.

SQUAD NO: 33

POSITION: Defender

DoB: 13 April 1994

SIGNED FROM: Came through the Hammers Academy

PREVIOUS CLUBS: Colchester Utd (loan), Portsmouth (loan)

INTERNATIONAL: England U18 and USA U20

WEST HAM UNITED

This season began badly but ended well.

The opening day brought a 4-0 thumping at Manchester City where Dennis Tueart, Rodney Marsh with two, and Mike Doyle did the damage.

There were 23,182 at the first home game 48 hours later when Frank Lampard and Billy Bonds scored as Luton Town left empty handed. That would be the only win in the opening seven league games though, five of which were lost.

Suddenly the Hammers went goal crazy beating Leicester City 6-2 and Birmingham City 3-0 at the Boleyn Ground before putting five past Burnley at Turf Moor. Billy Jennings would score in all of those games and finish his first season at the Club as top scorer with 13 League goals plus one in the League Cup.

The League Cup would bring another six goal haul against Tranmere Rovers before Fulham ended the Hammers' cup hopes. Later in the season, though, it would be West Ham's turn to end Fulham's hopes in the FA Cup.

ANSWER ON PAGE 82

SPOT THE SEASON

BACK ROW: Keith Robson, Clyde Best, Trevor Brooking, Billy Bonds, Bobby Ferguson, Mervyn Day, Kevin Lock, Pat Holland, John McDowell, Mike McGiven.

FRONT ROW: Tommy Taylor, Keith Coleman, Bobby Gould, Frank Lampard, Alan Taylor, Graham Paddon, Billy Jennings.

2014 QUIZ OF THE YEAR

Fancy yourself as an expert on the Hammers?

Try this quiz on 2014 and see how high up the table you can go. There are 20 questions - the same as the number of teams in the Barclays Premier League. Get all 20 questions right and you earn first place in the table. Get them all wrong and you'll be bottom. You lose one place for every incorrect answer you give, so get one wrong and be second, two wrong and be third and so on. Can you better the team's finishing position? Find the answers on page 82.

1

Who scored West Ham's goal at Old Trafford on 27 September?

6

Who were the two Italian players signed on loan on 25 January?

2

Against whom did Enner Valencia score his first Barclays Premier League goal?

4

When West Ham beat Sampdoria in August, which trophy did they win?

7

Matt Jarvis and Stewart Downing scored in the final six minutes of the summer's first friendly - who were the opponents?

9

Who scored West Ham's first Barclays U21 Premier League goal of the 2014/15 season?

3

Against whom was West Ham's first win of the calendar year?

5

Who was the 17-year-old who scored the last-minute winner in that game?

8

Who scored West Ham's first Barclays Premier League goal of the 2014/15 season?

10

Against which club did Diego Poyet make his first Barclays Premier League start?

11 Modibo Maiga joined which French side on a season-long loan?

13 Who was bought from Marseille in the summer?

12 Who joined the Hammers on a season-long loan from Arsenal?

14 Enner Valencia scored three goals for Ecuador at the summer's FIFA World Cup in Brazil, but against whom?

16 West Ham won four games in succession in February. Who were the vanquished clubs?

15 When Sam Allardyce won the Manager of the Month award for February, how many times had he won the award?

17 Which was the only club of the beaten quartet to score against West Ham in that run?

19 Name the four players who started the first six Barclays Premier League games of this season.

18 Who was bought from Ipswich Town in August?

20 Including this season, how many seasons have West Ham United spent in the top flight since the start of the Premier League era?

UP THE IRONS

WEST HAM AND THE FIRST WORLD WAR

Although other sports ground to a halt in the First World War, which Great Britain entered on 4 August 1914, professional football continued and despite much criticism, the 1914/15 season was not only started, it was completed. West Ham finished fourth in the First Division of the Southern League with goal machine Syd Puddefoot the star of the team.

While the Southern League and Football League ceased in 1915, football continued in the capital with London Principal, Supplementary and Combination Leagues. Indeed, West Ham's fine form throughout the war years is thought to have contributed to the Club being admitted to the Football League when it resumed in 1919. By 1923 West Ham had reached the First Division and played in the first-ever Wembley FA Cup Final.

Footballing glories of course paled into insignificance while the Great War was unfolding. Frederick Charrington of the famous brewing family was amongst those vehement in their criticism of football's continued presence. Charrington berated West Ham's players for cowardly playing football for money while men were dying on the continent.

While by and large the players kept playing, tens of thousands of people of course joined up. Of special interest to West Ham was the 13th service Battalion of The Essex Regiment. Predominantly consisting of people from West Ham supporting areas such as: Barking, Bow, Stepney, Silvertown and Leyton, the battalion became known as 'The West Ham Pals'. Arriving in France in December 1915, 'The West Ham Pals' made their first trench raid on 1 June 1916 and fought on the Somme, at Ypres, Cambrai and Vimy Ridge. 'Up the Irons' was known to be the battle-cry of the battalion.

On Remembrance Sunday in November 2009, Sir Trevor Brooking attended the unveiling of a memorial plaque to 'The West Ham Pals.'

Despite the criticism levelled at them, many footballers left their clubs to join the forces. West Ham goalkeeper Joe Webster joined what became known as The Footballers' Battalion, featuring some well known, often maverick characters such as England centre forward Tim Coleman. Another to join up was England international Jack Tresadern, who would become a lieutenant in the Royal Garrison Artillery and later go on to play for West Ham in the 1923 FA Cup final. While Tresadern was able to play successfully after the war, others were not so fortunate.

COUNTY BOROUGH OF WEST HAM

13TH (SERVICE) BATTN. ESSEX REGT. (WEST HAM.)

JOIN THE "HAMMERS" AND HAMMER THE HUNS

PRELIMINARY TRAINING IN THE BOROUGH

Apply 22, GROVE CRESCENT ROAD, or any Recruiting Office.

HENRY DYER,
Town Hall, West Ham.

SYD PUDDEFOOT

Five West Ham footballers were killed in action: William Kennedy, Frank Cannon, Fred Griffiths, Arthur Stallard and William Jones.

Two other players suffered horribly. Fred Harrison was gassed on the Western Front and never played football again. A similar fate befell George Hilsden, ironically nicknamed 'Gatling Gun George' before the war, because of how rapidly and often he fired goalwards. He and his brother Jack both played for West Ham. George had two spells with West Ham before the outbreak of war, either side of a goal-laden six years with Chelsea for whom he scored five goals on his debut and almost exactly two for every three of the 150 games he played for them. Hilsden scored 35 goals in 92 Southern League appearances in his second spell at West Ham and appeared in a further four war-time games. An England international who bagged an astonishing 14 goals in just eight games for his country, eight of those goals came on England's first overseas tour in 1908. Within the space of five days in June of that year 'Gatling Gun George' scored twice in an 11 (eleven)-1 win over Austria in Vienna, bagged four in a 7-0 thrashing of Hungary in Budapest and finished with another two in a 4-0 win over Bohemia in Prague. Little was he to know that less than a decade after starring on England's first foreign tour he would be representing his country on the battlefield. Hilsden suffered a mustard gas attack at Arras in 1917. He played for a short time for Chatham Town after the war but his career was effectively ended.

Being able to play or watch football became of relatively little concern as the horrors of the Great War unfolded. However, once the war was over, the joys of being able to come together in sport - and in years to come enjoy competitive club, as well as international football against teams from other countries - illustrated not only the futility of war but the healing powers that a shared worldwide love of sport can help to provide.

WEST HAM UNITED IN WORLD WAR ONE

1914-15, SOUTHERN LEAGUE

P	W	D	L	F	A	Pts	Pos
38	18	9	11	58	47	45	4th

1915-16   LONDON PRINCIPAL

P	W	D	L	F	A	Pts	Pos
22	10	4	8	47	35	24	4

LONDON SUPPLEMENTARY

P	W	D	L	F	A	Pts	Pos
14	9	2	3	32	16	20	2

1916-17 · LONDON LEAGUE

P	W	D	L	F	A	Pts	Pos
40	30	5	5	110	45	65	1

1917-18 · LONDON LEAGUE

P	W	D	L	F	A	Pts	Pos
36	20	9	7	103	51	49	2

1918-19

P	W	D	L	F	A	Pts	Pos
36	17	7	12	65	51	41	3

The Football League, with West Ham admitted, resumed in 1919-20.

WEST HAM UNITED FOOTBALLERS KILLED IN ACTION IN WORLD WAR ONE

WILLIAM KENNEDY

Killed in action on 13 October 1915.

A Lance Corporal in the London Scottish Regiment, William Kennedy's body was never found. His name appears on the memorial at Loos. Kennedy was a schoolteacher born in 1890. He signed for West Ham as a centre forward in 1910 and scored on his debut against Brighton & Hove Albion. That would be the first of ten goals from 23 appearances, the last of which was a career ending injury in an FA Cup second round replay at Middlesbrough on 2 February 2012. Eight days short of four years before he would lose his life he had enjoyed his greatest day as a player with a hat-trick against Brentford.

FRANK CANNON

Killed in action on the Western Front at Ypres on 15 February 1916.

Having joined the Bedfordshire, and later, the Essex Regiment, Frank became a Sergeant-Major. He is buried in Potijze Cemetery in Belgium. Frank had attracted West Ham's attention by scoring a hat-trick against the Club for QPR on 20 April 1908 as he helped Rangers to the Southern League Championship. Moving to West Ham he debuted on 1 October 1910, scored on his second appearance and played twice more.

FRED GRIFFITHS

Killed in action on the Western Front on 30 October 1917.

A Sergeant in the 15th battalion, Sherwood Foresters. A goalkeeper signed from Tottenham Hotspur in 1902 he would spend two years at West Ham before moving on to Gillingham, then known as New Brompton. Griffiths was a Wales international. He debuted against Scotland at Aberdeen in 1900 and then played against England at Cardiff a month later.

ARTHUR STALLARD

Killed in action on 30 November 1917.

A member of the London Regiment. Hackney-born, Arthur scored on his West Ham debut in a 3-2 away win over Millwall on 14 April 1914. Arthur evidently liked facing Millwall, in April 1916 he scored five goals in a friendly against them. In total he scored 17 goals in 23 war-time games in addition to his impressive tally of eight goals in 13 peace-time matches.

WILLIAM JONES

Killed in action on 6 May 1918.

A member of the Royal Welsh Fusiliers, Jones lost his life in Macedonia and is buried in Doiran Military cemetery which lies on the south east shore of Lake Doiran in the north of Greece.

A Wales international, he won four caps, the first two while he was with West Ham in 1901/02. In February 1902 he debuted against Scotland at Wrexham and played against England at Newcastle a month later. The following season he faced England at Wrexham and Scotland at Greenock.

'We will remember them'

WEST HAM UNITED

Which season do you think this picture comes from?

You'll find the answer on page 82, but see if you can work it out.

Another fantastically famous player who played, but isn't on the photo because he arrived during this season from Spurs, is Jimmy Greaves. In the back row, you have also got Clyde Best in his first season in the squad, while in the front row on the left as you look is Johnny Sissons, a scorer in the 1964 FA Cup Final. Of the 'keepers, the man in the middle is Steve Death who would play just once for the Hammers but become a legend at Reading where he played in over 500 matches.

The opening day of the campaign saw 33,300 witness a Geoff Hurst winner get the better of Newcastle at the Boleyn Ground. Hurst and Greaves would notch a brace each in a 5-1 win away to Manchester City who had earlier won 4-0 at West Ham.

This season saw West Ham finish 17th out of 22 in the top flight. Everton were champions, finishing eight points ahead of runners-up Leeds in the days of two points for a win. Cup competitions provided little joy. Instant elimination from the FA Cup came at Middlesbrough while defeat was suffered at Nottingham Forest in the League Cup after a 4-2 home win over Halifax Town in the second round.

Ok then, cover up the names of the players and see how many you can name.

There are some gigantic figures in Hammers' history on this photo. World Cup icons Bobby Moore, Geoff Hurst and Martin Peters for starters, plus Trevor Brooking ...and have you spotted Harry Redknapp yet?

SPOT
THE SEASON

Back Row: Billy Bonds, Paul Heffer, Alan Stephenson, Peter Bennett, Clyde Best, Bobby Moore, John Cushley.
Middle Row: Martin Peters, John Charles, Peter Grotier, Stephen Death, Bobby Ferguson, Frank Lampard, Trevor Brooking.
Front Row: Harry Redknapp, Ron Boyce, Geoff Hurst, Jimmy Lindsay, Bobby Howe, John Sissons.

31

Champions of the Championship, Cardiff City arrived at the Boleyn Ground on the opening day of the season for their first-ever game in the Barclays Premier League.

Looking to emulate their Wales rivals Swansea City's success, they would be buoyant and difficult first day opponents, but an early goal from Joe Cole and a fairly late one from Kevin Nolan got the season off to a fine start with new boy Stewart Downing making his debut in front of an almost capacity Boleyn Ground.

2013/14 REVIEW

The bright start unfortunately soon lost its shine with three games without a goal, followed by two defeats, meaning that going into the seventh Barclays Premier League game of the season at White Hart Lane the Hammers lay in 16th place as the embryonic table began to take shape.

In contrast, West Ham visited a Tottenham side sitting in second place after four wins, one defeat and a draw with Chelsea in their first six fixtures. The match would prove to be one of the highlights of the season as three goals in 13 glorious second -half minutes produced an emphatic 3-0 win.

The rout began with Winston Reid's only goal of the season. Six minutes after Reid broke the deadlock in the 66th minute, Ricardo Vaz Te struck to double the lead and with Spurs rattled, Ravel Morrison completed the scoring with the Hammers Goal of the Season with eleven minutes to go.

It was the first West Ham win at White Hart Lane since 1999 and well worth the wait.

West Ham were 17th as Fulham were welcomed at the end of November. A goal from Mohamed Diame nudged the Hammers ahead just after the break with two goals in the final ten minutes from Carlton and then Joe Cole resulting in the second 3-0 win of the season.

Carlton Cole had been out of the picture for much of the year. Informed he was being released on 22 May he had been re-signed on 14 October following injury to £15m summer signing Andy Carroll. This was Cole's first goal after his return.

By the time the return fixture was lost on New Year's Day at Craven Cottage, only two points had been taken from six games, a well-earned point at Swansea City and a goalless draw at home to struggling Sunderland, leaving the Hammers second bottom in the Barclays Premier League.

The following Sunday, with top-flight survival taking priority, Sam Allardyce fielded a youthful side, giving valuable experience to debutants Danny Whitehead, Callum Driver and Sebastian Lletget, as well as handing George Moncur his first start, in the 5-0 FA Cup third round exit at Nottingham Forest. Three days later Manchester City turned on the style, running out 6-0 winners in the Capital One Cup semi-final first-leg at the Etihad Stadium.

A reaction was needed and it came in the next game when the season's opening fixture against Cardiff City was reversed. The result however wasn't, with a repeat of the first day's 2-0 victory, this time Carlton Cole's goal being added to in the last minute by Mark Noble's only goal from open play all season.

It was brief respite as everyone at the Club was brought back down to earth with a 3-1 defeat at home to Newcastle where the consolation was Carlton Cole scored for the fourth time in six Barclays Premier League games.

Also impressing at the other end of the pitch was Adrian in goal. Having kept a clean sheet when brought into the side at Cardiff, he made it two shut-outs in three games with a defiant show at Stamford Bridge where Jose Mourinho had plenty to say as Sam Allardyce's side left with a point from a goalless draw.

Chelsea recorded 39 efforts on goal, the most any side had produced without scoring since 2003/04, but the visitors' resilience - even when down to ten men after losing Joey O'Brien through a dislocated shoulder - earned a tenth clean sheet of the season, a record which only Arsenal could equal. Moreover it would be the first of four successive clean sheets, the first time since 1985 that it had been achieved at this level.

Mr. Mourinho wasn't impressed by West Ham pulling up the drawbridge at the Bridge, describing the Hammers' performance as 'nineteenth century football.' Sam Allardyce was not remotely bothered, "He can tell me all he wants, I don't care" smiled Sam, before adding, "I love to see Chelsea players moaning at the referee, trying to intimidate him, Jose jumping up and down and saying we play rubbish football.

"It's brilliant when you get a result against him"

It would be West Ham's last draw until 15 September and the confidence and belief gained from it would lead to a sensational run of four successive victories, lifting the team from a relegation position to the top ten!

All four of the victories would be by two goals, with only a single goal conceded and Kevin Nolan notching five of his season's tally of seven goals. Unsurprisingly the capture of 12 points out of 12 brought Sam Allardyce the February Manager of the Month award, the fifth such award of the gaffer's career.

Three defeats followed the quartet of wins. There was, however, a silver lining in the shape of Andy Carroll's first goal since his transfer, but after 30 games gone the club had come to rest in 14th place.

An own goal and a penalty brought a welcome win at home to Hull City before another Carroll goal sparked a 2-1 win at Sunderland.

The season though would taper off with four defeats in a row, victory in the penultimate match and final day defeat at Manchester City who clinched the title after a 2-0 win, much more respectable than the Capital One Cup semi-final defeat on the same ground.

Pleasingly, the win in the penultimate game registered a 'double' over Spurs. In fact, it was a 'treble' as Tottenham had also been beaten in the quarter-final of the Capital One Cup.

A 2-1 win at White Hart Lane was the highlight of a cup run that began with a win over Cheltenham, continued with a win over Cardiff - another side beaten three times in the season - and an away win at promotion-bound Burnley. The run ended with a semi-final defeat by Manchester City who added a 3-0 second leg win at the Boleyn Ground to their emphatic first-leg.

It had been a season where the highs and lows came in batches but in the second season after promotion, in the cold light of day, 13th place and a run to a cup semi-final represented a turbulent campaign that had some excellent days.

DYLAN TOMBIDES

This book is about the things that matter to West Ham fans, the players, the games and the club. For many a fan their lives revolve around the events at E13 9AZ. Sometimes, something happens, that stops you in your tracks and puts the wins, defeats and draws into perspective. Such an occasion occurred on April 18th 2014. It doesn't matter who West Ham were playing on or near that date because on that day West Ham lost something much more precious than a football match. It was the day 20-year-old Dylan Tombides passed away.

Dylan had fought a three-year battle after being diagnosed with testicular cancer. The diagnosis came about during the 2011 Under-17 World Cup where Perth-born Dylan was representing Australia, who he played for at U17 and U23 level. A very talented player and a great character, Dylan drew upon all of his resources in his battle with the disease. In June 2012 there was delight when it appeared that Dylan had won his greatest battle having been informed he was back to full health.

Apparently clear of the disease he was allowed back to full training and impressed so much that he made his debut on September 9th 2012 as a substitute in the Capital One Cup against Wigan. Having been an unused substitute in the Barclays Premier League at Sunderland in May 2011 it seemed that Tombides was back on track in his quest to forge a successful career in the game he gave so much to.

Tragically, the cancer returned and Dylan passed away with his parents Jim and Tracylee by his side, along with his beloved brother Taylor, who remains an Academy player with West Ham. In Dylan's honour the club retired his shirt number 38, a distinction Dylan shares with Bobby Moore.

At the time of Dylan's death the club issued the following statement:

"Dylan's amazing resilience and positivity saw him through months of surgery and chemotherapy, while his outstanding talent saw him make his first team debut in a League Cup tie with Wigan at the Boleyn Ground in September 2012.

"Away from the pitch Dylan did a huge amount of work to raise awareness of male cancer, supporting the 'One for the Boys' campaign at a number of high profile events alongside the likes of Hollywood star Samuel L. Jackson, snooker star Jimmy White and fellow Australian Peter Andre.

"Dylan was respected by everyone who knew him for his intelligent views on the game and his larger than life character. He was a loving son, amazing brother and well-respected member of the West Ham squad. He will be hugely missed by everyone who had the honour of knowing him.

"His passing will be marked by a minute's applause ahead of Saturday's Barclays Premier League game with Crystal Palace at the Boleyn Ground. The Hammers' players will also wear black armbands in his memory. The thoughts of everyone associated with the club are with his parents Tracylee and Jim, brother Taylor, his family and friends at this sad time. The club request that their privacy is now respected and they are allowed to grieve their much loved son and brother in peace."

2013/14
HAMMER
OF THE YEAR

MARK **NOBLE**

2012/13	**Winston Reid**
2011/12	Mark Noble
2010/11	**Scott Parker**
2009/10	Scott Parker
2008/09	**Scott Parker**
2007/08	Robert Green
2006/07	**Carlos Tevez**
2005/06	Danny Gabbidon
2004/05	**Teddy Sheringham**
2003/04	Matthew Etherington
2002/03	**Joe Cole**
2001/02	Sebastien Schemmel
2000/01	**Stuart Pearce**
1999/00	Paolo Di Canio
1998/99	**Shaka Hislop**
1997/98	Rio Ferdinand
1996/97	**Julian Dicks**
1995/96	Julian Dicks
1994/95	**Steve Potts**
1993/94	Trevor Morley
1992/93	**Steve Potts**
1991/92	Julian Dicks
1990/91	**Ludek Miklosko**
1989/90	Julian Dicks
1988/89	**Paul Ince**
1987/88	Stewart Robson
1986/87	**Billy Bonds**
1985/86	Tony Cottee
1984/85	**Paul Allen**
1983/84	Trevor Brooking
1982/83	**Alvin Martin**
1981/82	Alvin Martin
1980/81	**Phil Parkes**
1979/80	Alvin Martin
1978/79	**Alan Devonshire**
1977/78	Trevor Brooking
1976/77	**Trevor Brooking**
1975/76	Trevor Brooking
1974/75	**Billy Bonds**
1973/74	Billy Bonds
1972/73	**Bryan Robson**
1971/72	Trevor Brooking
1970/71	**Billy Bonds**
1969/70	Bobby Moore
1968/69	**Geoff Hurst**
1967/68	Bobby Moore
1966/67	**Geoff Hurst**
1965/66	Geoff Hurst
1964/65	**Martin Peters**
1963/64	Johnny Byrne
1962/63	**Bobby Moore**
1961/62	Lawrie Leslie
1960/61	**Bobby Moore**
1959/60	Malcolm Musgrove
1958/59	**Ken Brown**
1957/58	Andy Malcolm

99/00
59/60
90/91
62/63
00/01
71/72
86/87
72/73
97/98
81/82
02/03
85/86

NEW STADIUM

2014 has been another eventful year for West Ham United away from the football pitch, as momentum builds towards an exciting future at the Club's new Stratford home.

Over at Queen Elizabeth Olympic Park, the Stadium's conversion into a state-of-the-art football venue continues apace, with the magnificent roof set for completion in spring 2015.

While the site will be a hive of activity over the coming months, the most significant changes will follow the 2015 Rugby World Cup matches next autumn, when the proud home of the Hammers will really begin to take shape.

STADIUM TIMELINE

January 2015
Will offer the first glimpse of the new football ready, floodlight configuration and the lion's share of the internal transformation will take place this year, with the installation of the turnstiles, catering and bathroom facilities.

Summer 2015
Turnstiles, catering and bathroom facilities all complete.

Spring 2016
The Stadium will start to look and feel like the home of West Ham United inside and out with the superior hospitality lounges, Club Megastore and Ticket Office all approaching completion.

May 2016
West Ham United bid a final farewell to the Boleyn Ground.

Summer 2016
The site will be proudly displaying West Ham United colours, inside and out, as a celebratory series of pre-season events take place ahead of the 2016/17 season kick-off.

ON THE HORIZON

PARK LIFE

Over the past 12 months, many a West Ham player has made the short trip to the former OIympic Stadium to size up the spectacular venue.

Back in April, Matt Jarvis and Carlton Cole were on hand to herald the complete re-opening of Queen Elizabeth Olympic Park, when the newly-landscaped south of the Park opened its doors to the general public for the first time since the Olympic and Paralympic Games.

Designed by James Corner Field Operations, the south of the Park features an action-packed adventure playground, interactive water fountains and four themed walking trails exploring the key sights of London 2012.

Together with eight iconic Olympic venues, the beautiful parklands and waterways amount to the perfect day-out destination. Cole, meanwhile, was certainly impressed by the outstanding view.

"It's a really exciting time for the Olympic Park," the No.24 confirmed. "The fact that it is opening to the public is a great thing for London and it's a new adventure for Londoners as well. It will be booming over here in the summer and I'm really looking forward to it."

ENNER EXCITED BY 'DREAM SWITCH'

Summer signing Enner Valencia needed little time to take a shine to the world-renowned Stratford venue, as he held his first Club press conference at Queen Elizabeth Olympic Park in August.

Fresh from his goalscoring exploits at the FIFA World Cup with Ecuador, the 24-year-old said it would be a dream come true to fire the Hammers into Europe come the Club's move to the former Olympic Stadium in 2016.

"Being so close to the Stadium I just want to go inside and start playing. I saw the Olympics on television, but I never dreamed of standing here and one day I'm looking forward to playing in this great Stadium," he confirmed. "It played a big part in me coming to West Ham.

"It would be fantastic [to be in Europe] and a dream come true. Hopefully we can make it happen in a couple of years."

WATCH OUR NEW HOME BEING BUILT

Supporters can keep track of developments at the Stadium wherever they are! A new time-lapse portal allows fans to watch images from Queen Elizabeth Olympic Park to see the conversion taking shape for themselves.

Working with our partners at the London Legacy Development Corporation, high-resolution time-lapse cameras have been installed to take regular pictures of the work in progress.

Two of the cameras are located in the heart of the new Stadium, providing a close-up look at how the old structure is changing to accommodate the huge cantilevered roof, a new floodlighting system, the innovative retractable seating and our state-of-the-art Desso pitch.

Camera one takes in the view from the South Stand towards the North, while camera two offers a view across the Stadium taking in the East Stand, which will feature 'kop style' seating. A third camera is located high up in the ArcelorMittal Orbit, towering above Queen Elizabeth Olympic Park and the city skyline. It provides a dramatic bird's eye view of all the work in progress in and around the Stadium.

WEST HAM UNITED LAUNCH CLUB LONDON

West Ham United proudly announced the launch of Club London in September, offering supporters the opportunity to watch their heroes from London's newest and most spectacularly located members club in the heart of Queen Elizabeth Olympic Park.

The VIP areas are all to be located in the West Stand of the newly-reconfigured Stadium, delivering unrivalled hospitality and entertainment experiences in the Barclays Premier League.

The launch coincided with the opening of a dedicated Reservation Centre in Westfield, just a short walk from the Stadium.

There, every current Corporate Member and Season Ticket Holder will be offered a dedicated appointment with an advisor to help them choose the right seat for their needs and budget.

Speaking of the launch, Vice Chairman Karren Brady CBE said: "This is an incredibly exciting milestone for us as it is the first announcement on the way to revealing all of our world-class plans for the new Stadium. The details released today show that we have been true to our word, in that the new-look Stadium will look and feel like West Ham's home.

"We can't reveal everything at this stage, though, as we want a visit to the Reservation Centre to be a truly memorable experience for our supporters when they attend for their individual appointments, so there will also be a few more surprises in store for them."

THE NEW STADIUM IN NUMBERS

As things stand, the 54,000 capacity will be the third highest in English club football.

The transformation will use 5,500 tonnes of steel and 6km of cabling.

5,000 people will have worked two million hours on the transformation project once it is complete.

With a total size of 45,000m² and 84m at its deepest point, the Stadium will have the longest cantilevered roof in the world, weighing 4,500 tonnes.

The roof will cover 100 per cent of seats in the ground, compared to the 40 per cent left uncovered in the 2012 Stadium.

The 105m x 68m pitch will be comparable to the size of the pitches at Wembley, the Emirates, the Etihad Stadium and Old Trafford.

There will be 995 toilets, 35 catering outlets and 92 turnstiles.

Back Row: Kirkup, Lansdowne, Bond, Dwyer, Gregory, Rhodes, Brown, Cantwell, Moore.
Front Row: Wragg, Woosnam, Grice, Keeble, Dick, Musgrove, Malcolm, Obeney.

44

Starting the season with an away win at Portsmouth, newly-promoted West Ham beat reigning champions Wolves in their opening home game and then walloped Aston Villa 7-2 in the third fixture.

By the time they had beaten Manchester United in their sixth game, in a match which marked the debut of Bobby Moore, the Hammers topped the table.

It was a great season and when fans returned home from seeing Spurs beaten 2-1 at the Boleyn Ground on Christmas Day, (yes, they played on Christmas Day back then), they probably thought things could not get any better. They were wrong, West Ham beat Spurs 4-1 at White Hart Lane on Boxing Day! A 5-1 home win over Manchester City in the last home league game of the season left West Ham third, and while they slipped to sixth after a last day loss at Leeds, it was still the Club's highest ever league position.

Four players: John Bond, Noel Cantwell, Andy Malcolm and Hammer of the Year Ken Brown, were ever-presents. Top scorer John Dick netted 27 times with Vic Keeble getting 20. No one else got into double figures.

Can you spot the season?

Find the answer on page 82.

SPOT THE SEASON

WEST HAM UNITED

45

FA CUP FINALS

WEST HAM UNITED 0 BOLTON WANDERERS 2 — 1923

Arguably the only Final most famous for something other than a player or a manager. The first-ever Wembley final is still known as 'The White Horse Final' after a police officer called Constable George Scorey became conspicuous on a majestic 13-year-old white horse named Billy in clearing what is still a record crowd for a football match in England. An amazing 126,047 poured into the new stadium to see the Hammers play Bolton Wanderers, who took the lead through David Jack, with West Ham temporarily down to ten men at the time. There was not an injury, a defender was simply trying to get through the overflowing crowd and back into the action having taken a throw in! Jack Smith ensured the trophy travelled north with a screamer of a second goal eight minutes into the second half but there was ample compensation for West Ham, who gained promotion to the First Division for the first time.

HAMMERS: Hufton, Henderson, Young, Bishop, Kay, Tresadern, Richards, Brown, Watson, Moore, Ruffell.

WEST HAM UNITED 3 PRESTON NORTH END 2 — 1964

Seven players with a surname beginning with B, led by Footballer of the Year Bobby Moore, won the Cup for the first time. The Hammers had been in the Second Division when they had reached their only previous FA Cup Final, but this time it was opponents Preston who were in Division Two. Preston, with 17-year-old Howard Kendall in their line-up, took an early lead through Doug Holden but within a minute 18-year-old John Sissons restored parity with a great goal after he beat two defenders to score West Ham's first ever goal in an FA Cup final. Half-time would be a time of worry, however, as Preston regained the lead five minutes before the break, courtesy of Alec Dawson who had also been instrumental in their first.

Two years later Geoff Hurst's World Cup final hat-trick would include a goal the West German opponents argued had not crossed the line. On this occasion Hurst equalised with a header that hit the bar and then trickled just over the line as North End 'keeper Alan Kelly desperately tried to keep it out. FA Cup finals thrive on drama and a thrilling game climaxed in the dying seconds when Ron Boyce headed the winner from a Peter Brabrook cross. The Cup belonged to Ron Greenwood's Hammers.

HAMMERS: Standen, Bond, Burkett, Bovington, Brown, Moore, Brabrook, Boyce, Byrne, Hurst, Sissons.

WEST HAM UNITED 2 FULHAM 0 — 1975

In a quirk of fate Bobby Moore lined up as part of Second Division Fulham's only FA Cup final side against the Club he had given such service to and won the Cup with eleven years earlier.

Twenty-one-year old Alan Taylor was the hero of this triumph. Having already scored both goals in both the semi and quarter-finals he produced another brace beneath the twin towers, following up on shots Cottagers' 'keeper Peter Mellor spilled from Billy Jennings and Graham Paddon.

HAMMERS: Day, McDowell, T. Taylor, Lock, Lampard, Bonds, Paddon, Brooking, Jennings, A. Taylor, Holland.

WEST HAM UNITED 1 ARSENAL 0 — 1980

Trevor Brooking was a player blessed with the silkiest skills but heading was not renowned as one of them. Brooking had only ever netted with two headers but had been saving one up for this biggest of days as a player known for his brain power used his head to score the only goal of the final after just 13 minutes.

The Gunners had become the first club to reach a third successive final in the twentieth century but West Ham were winning the trophy for the second time in five years.

These days a red card is an automatic punishment for denying a clear goal-scoring opportunity. Willie Young's cynical chopping down of Paul Allen, when the youngest player to appear in a final (17 years, 256 days) was bearing down on goal, was an incident that led to the modern day sanction.

HAMMERS: Parkes, Stewart, Lampard, Bonds, Martin, Devonshire, Allen, Pearson, Cross, Brooking, Pike.

WEST HAM UNITED 3 LIVERPOOL 3 — 2006

Lost 1-3 on penalties

West Ham had won the cup with an injury time goal in 1964 but that did not make Steven Gerrard's 35-yard injury-time equaliser any easier to stomach, especially after West Ham had led 2-0 and 3-2. The Merseysiders went on to win on penalties as they had a year earlier after recovering from 3-0 down against AC Milan in the UEFA Champions League Final.

This FA Cup Final was the last to be played outside of England at Cardiff's Millennium Stadium while Wembley was rebuilt. The Hammers went ahead when Jamie Carragher turned Lionel Scaloni's cross into his own goal after 21 minutes. Dean Ashton soon doubled the lead but before West Ham could settle on it, Djibril Cisse pulled one back. West Ham however, led at half-time.

Gerrard levelled nine minutes into the second-half but nine minutes later Paul Konchesky's cross deceived Pepe Reina in the Liverpool goal to restore the Hammers' advantage. So it remained until Gerrard's rescue act, which took the match to extra-time followed by a penalty shoot-out.

Only substitute Teddy Sheringham could convert for West Ham with Bobby Zamora, Konchesky and Anton Ferdinand all unable to score, while for Liverpool, although Sami Hyypia failed with their second attempt, Didi Hamman, Steven Gerrard and John Arne Riise all beat Shaka Hislop.

HAMMERS: Hislop, Scaloni, A. Ferdinand, Gabbidon, Konchesky, Benayoun, Reo-Coker, Fletcher (Dailly 77) Etherington (Sheringham 85), Harewood, Ashton (Zamora 71).

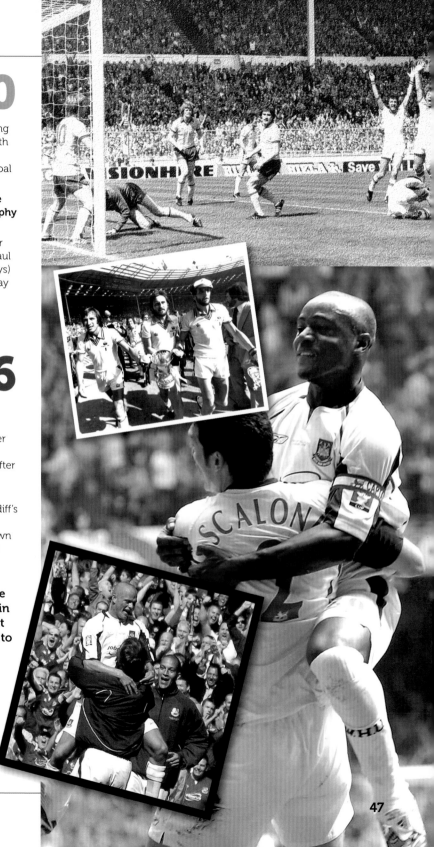

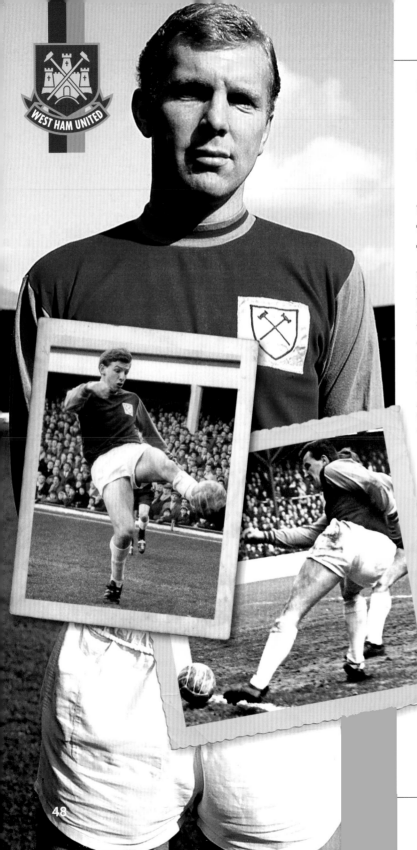

LEAGUE CUPFINALS

WEST HAM UNITED 2
WBA 1

1966

Having played in the first ever cup final at Wembley (in the FA Cup in 1923) the Irons have since twice managed to play in the last cup finals before they were switched to Wembley. Once was in the 2006 FA Cup Final, in the last of the Millennium Stadium finals before the new Wembley was opened. The 1966 League Cup Final was the other occasion, this was the last of the two-legged finals.

Having lifted the FA Cup in 1964 and the European Cup Winners' Cup in 1965, West Ham were after a cup hat-trick. They missed out on the League Cup - but 'won the World Cup' instead of course!

A crowd of 28,323 attended the Boleyn Ground for the first-leg of the final but were dismayed to see Albion's Jeff Astle put the visitors ahead early in the second-half. West Ham were to level in the 72nd minute with a volley from out wide from Bobby Moore, who like Paul Konchesky in the 2006 FA Cup Final, fortuitously found the back of the net. Johnny Byrne made it 2-1 in the 90th minute but sadly there was a second-leg still to play at the Hawthorns, which would prove prickly.

HAMMERS: Standen, Burnett, Burkett, Peters, Brown, Moore, Brabrook, Boyce, Byrne, Hurst, Dear.

SECOND LEG

WBA 4
WEST HAM UNITED 1

(Aggregate WBA 5-3 West Ham United)

It was a first-half to forget. Hammers 'keeper Jim Standen had to pick the ball out of his net four times before a half-time orange that would have had a bitter taste. While Martin Peters pulled a goal back quarter of an hour from time, Albion ran out 5-3 victors over the two legs.

An early goal from John Kaye levelled the aggregate score with Tony Brown nudging West Brom ahead in the 17th minute before a Clive Clarke header and a 30-yarder from skipper Graham Williams had the 31,925 Baggies 'boing- boinging.'

HAMMERS: Standen, Burnett, Bovington, Peters, Brown, Moore, Brabrook, Boyce, Byrne, Hurst, Sissons.

WEST HAM UNITED 1
LIVERPOOL 1

1981

100,000 had witnessed a goalless 117 minutes when Liverpool looked to have broken Hammers' hearts when Alan Kennedy - that Anfield full back with a penchant for cup final goals - scored at the second attempt after his free kick came back to him off the West Ham wall.

Nowadays it would be considered a good goal but in 1981 it was offside. Even the linesman thought so as he flagged that Sammy Lee was in an offside position. The referee though was Clive Thomas, never a stranger to controversy, and he awarded the goal.

With nothing to lose West Ham poured forward and from a corner, Liverpool's Terry McDermott punched the ball off the line from Alvin Martin's last minute goalbound header. A penalty was awarded.

Showing admirable composure Ray Stewart stepped up to score and level the match.

HAMMERS: Parkes, Stewart, Lampard, Bonds, Martin, Devonshire, Neighbour, Goddard (Pearson), Cross, Brooking, Pike.

REPLAY
WEST HAM UNITED 1
LIVERPOOL 2

Just over a third of the Wembley attendance, 36,693, reassembled at Villa Park for the replay two-and-a-half weeks after the initial meeting. The goals required patience in the first meeting but they came early in the replay.

Paul Goddard provided West Ham with a tenth minute advantage but two goals in three minutes just before the half-hour turned the tie. The equaliser came from a volley Kenny Dalglish struck from a narrow angle before an Alan Hansen header from a corner went in having clipped Billy Bonds.

West Ham had levelled after falling behind with two minutes of extra time to play at Wembley but here could find no way through in the hour after the final goal. Liverpool had their first League Cup but for West Ham the wait goes on to this day.

HAMMERS: Parkes, Stewart, Lampard, Bonds, Martin, Devonshire, Neighbour, Goddard, Cross, Brooking, Pike.

49

EUROPEAN FINALS

EUROPEAN CUP WINNERS' CUP
WEST HAM UNITED 2
TSV 1860 MUNICH 0
1965

Was this the greatest day in the history of West Ham United? 100,000 did not just pack Wembley to see West Ham become only the second English side to win a European trophy, they saw them do so with an exceptional performance of the finest football befitting the Academy of football.

West Ham had qualified for this competition by winning the FA Cup at the same stadium the previous season, but whereas on that occasion against Preston the result had been better than the performance, this time the two went hand in hand. The Hammers were missing key men Peter Brabrook and Johnny Byrne but there was no sign of any lack of cohesion in Ron Greenwood's side. Indeed it would be one of the players brought into the team who would grab both of the goals.

1860 were no mugs. They had scored 21 goals and conceded only four in reaching the final and played some good stuff of their own but just as a German side would lose the World Cup Final at Wembley a year later they ended the game well beaten. Munich were knocked out by the old one-two - two goals in three minutes. The deadlock was broken with 20 minutes to go, Alan Sealey slipping the ball home after taking a pass threaded though from Ronnie Boyce. Before the Germans could recover Sealey had made it two, pouncing when 'Perica' (as 'keeper Peter Radenkovic was known) made a mess of a cross from skipper Bobby Moore.

HAMMERS: Standen, Kirkup, Burkett, Peters, Brown, Moore, Sealey, Boyce, Hurst, Dear, Sissons.

EUROPEAN CUP WINNERS' CUP
WEST HAM UNITED 2
ANDERLECHT 4
1976

Playing the final against Anderlecht in their home city of Brussels was always going to be a tall order, though West Ham had had the advantage of Wembley in 1965.

And yet it was a case of so near and yet so far to a second major European trophy. Back in the mid-seventies the Cup Winners' Cup was second only to the European Cup in terms of prestige. West Ham were good value for a 29th minute lead provided by Pat Holland and had they got to half-time ahead perhaps the trophy would have been won. The Belgian side though were to receive the lift of a goal just before the break. It came from a mistake. Frank Lampard attempted to find 'keeper Mervyn Day but the ball was short and Peter Ressell (who had scored for Feyenoord against Spurs in the 1974 UEFA Cup Final) got there first to present a gift for Robbie Rensenbrink who had played in the previous World Cup final and would also play in the next. The scorer turned provider shortly after the re-start, teeing up future West Ham man Francois Van Der Elst, but West Ham were no pushovers. In the quarter-finals they'd trailed 4-0 at one stage but clawed their way back and here they drew level in the 66th minute.

The architect, as so often, was Trevor Brooking who provided a cross gleefully finished off by Keith Robson.

To their credit Anderlecht refused to be derailed. They had a top class, experienced side and their class told as Dutch internationals Ari Haan and Rensenbrink assumed control. Having had the ecstasy of scoring earlier, Holland ironically brought down Dutch international Rensenbrink in the box, the Dutchman tucking away the resulting spot-kick. Having scored twice, Rensenbrink duly produced a second assist, again Van Der Elst being the beneficiary of a through ball Brooking would have been proud of. Van der Elst still had work to do but skated past John McDowell and 'keeper Day before completing the scoring in front of a crowd of 51,296 inside the Heysel Stadium which just under a decade later would be the scene of the most tragic European Final of all when 39 people lost their lives at the European Cup Final between Liverpool and Juventus.

HAMMERS: Day, Coleman, Lampard (A. Taylor 47), Bonds, T. Taylor, McDowell, Holland, Paddon, Jennings, Brooking, Robson.

INTERTOTO CUP · FIRST LEG
WEST HAM UNITED 0
METZ 1

1999

The Intertoto Cup provided a route into the UEFA Cup for West Ham, Juventus and Montpellier who won the three Intertoto finals, Juventus beating Rennes and Montpellier edging out Hamburg on penalties.

It did not look like there would be UEFA Cup football at the Boleyn Ground when Frank Lampard failed to convert a penalty as French side Metz established a 1-0 lead before 25,372 in east London. The visitors' 12th minute goal-scorer would go on to become a familiar face in the Premier League, Louis Saha.

HAMMERS: Hislop, R. Ferdinand, Minto, Potts, Foe (Kitson 76), Lomas, Lampard, Moncur, Sinclair, Di Canio, Wanchope.

INTERTOTO CUP · SECOND LEG
METZ 1
WEST HAM UNITED 3
(Aggregate 3-2 to West Ham)

Overturning the first-leg deficit to lead on aggregate by the interval, West Ham called the tune at the Stade Saint-Symphorien where 19,599 saw Trevor Sinclair level things on aggregate with a left foot shot in the 24th minute. Two minutes before half-time Lampard atoned for his first-leg penalty aberration with a well taken goal.

The home side made it 2-2 on aggregate in the 68th minute, substitute Nenad Jestrovic netting twelve minutes after being introduced, but with twelve minutes to go Paolo Wanchope danced around the 'keeper to win the final 3-2 on aggregate.

HAMMERS: Hislop, R. Ferdinand, Potts, Foe, Lomas, Lampard, Moncur, Sinclair, Keller, Di Canio (J. Cole 79), Wanchope.

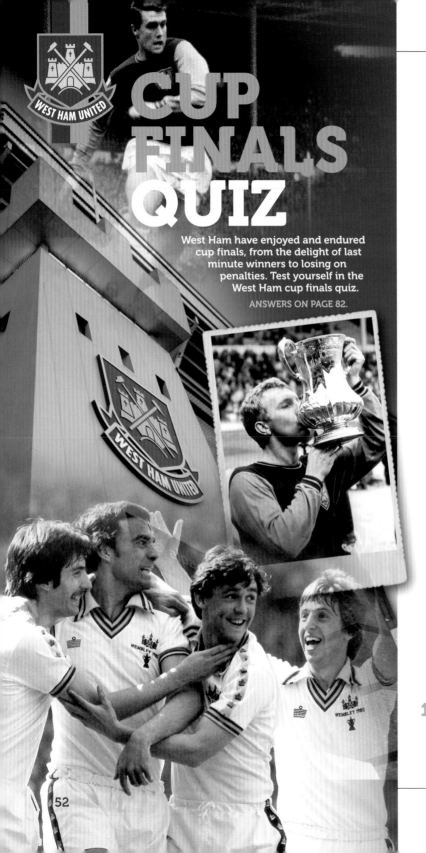

CUP FINALS QUIZ

West Ham have enjoyed and endured cup finals, from the delight of last minute winners to losing on penalties. Test yourself in the West Ham cup finals quiz.

ANSWERS ON PAGE 82.

1. Including replays and each leg of two-legged finals, how many games have West Ham played as cup finals?

2. Who scored West Ham's first-ever cup final goal?

3. How many times have West Ham played in cup finals at Wembley?

4. How many West Ham 'cup finals' have been played at the Boleyn Ground?

5. Name the players to have scored twice in a cup final for West Ham.

6. Name the players to have scored twice in a cup final against West Ham.

7. How many last-minute goals have West Ham scored in cup finals?

8. Name the odd one out: Pym, Kelly, Mellor, Jennings, Clemence, Reina.

9. Who came on as a substitute for West Ham at Wembley in the 1981 League Cup Final?

10. How many team changes did the Hammers make between the two legs of the 1966 League Cup Final?

52

11. **Adding together the scores of all of West Ham's cup finals, have the Hammers scored more than they have conceded, (excluding penalty shoot-outs)?**

12. Taking aggregate scores, where applicable, as one score, have West Ham won more or lost more of the cup finals they've contested?

13. **Who was the only Hammer to convert a penalty in the 2006 FA Cup Final shoot-out with Liverpool?**

14. What was the nickname of 1964 FA Cup Final match-winner Ronnie Boyce?

15. **Who kept goal for West Ham in the 1980 FA Cup Final?**

16. How many different countries have West Ham played cup finals in?

17. **How many of West Ham's 1966 World Cup winners scored in cup finals for West Ham?**

18. Excluding goals scored in a penalty shoot-out, who is the last Hammer to have scored for the Club in a cup final and also been Hammer of the Year.

19. **Who scored but also conceded a penalty in the 1976 European Cup Winners' Cup Final?**

20. What was the name of the white horse at the 1923 FA Cup Final?

JIMMY RUFFELL

THE 500 CLUB

ALL COMPETITIONS, INCLUDING MINOR ONES, ARE INCLUDED IN THE APPEARANCE TOTALS.

To play one game for West Ham would be a dream come true for thousands of people. Imagine what it is like to play 500 or more. Meet the members of the 500 club...

JIMMY **RUFFELL** 548

An England international winger, who won the first of his six caps for England alongside former West Ham centre forward Syd Puddefoot against Scotland, in April 1926 at Old Trafford. Known for his precise crosses, Doncaster-born Jimmy played in the 1923 FA Cup Final and was ever-present in both the 1924/25 and 1931/32 seasons.

Incredibly for a winger, as well as making many a goal he managed to score an astonishing 166 in Claret and Blue, and added one more in two appearances for Aldershot in 1937/38, after a 16-year career at the Boleyn Ground. Jimmy died aged 89 in 1989 and was West Ham's record appearance maker until being surpassed by Bobby Moore in 1973.

STEVE **POTTS** 505

Steve has been Hammer of the Year twice, once in 1994/95 and previously in the promotion year of 1992/93 when he was ever-present. He was also runner-up to Julian Dicks in 1991/92. A versatile defender, Steve captained the Club at every level and, although American-born gained England caps at youth level.

A 17-year-old debutant on New Year's Day 1985, his second game came the following season and his third the season after that when he played nine times, followed by eleven appearances in 1987/88 before starting to play regularly in 1988/89. In his 500 plus games Steve found the net just once, and that with the aid of a deflection, in a 7-1 Boleyn Ground mauling of the Tigers of Hull City. Steve's son Daniel is currently a member of the West Ham first-team squad.

VIC **WATSON** 505

Steve Potts scored just one goal in 505 games. Vic Watson scored 326 in the same number of appearances! It is almost impossible to believe that his record as the Club's record goalscorer will ever be beaten.

Like Geoff Hurst he once scored six goals in a game, in Vic's case against Leeds in February 1929 at the Boleyn Ground. He would score four goals in a game on three occasions and bang in 13 hat-tricks for good measure. In 1929/30 he netted 50 goals, his eight in the FA Cup included four against Leeds, they must have dreaded him!

Born in 1897, Vic died back in his home county of Cambridgeshire in 1988. He was capped five times by England, scoring four goals and finished his career with 14 goals in 36 games for Southampton in 1935/36.

HONOURABLE MENTIONS

SIR GEOFF **HURST** 499

Sometimes forwards are revered for one stellar occasion. Not even Pele or Maradona could match Geoff Hurst's World Cup Final hat-trick for England in 1966, but Hurst was not just a big-game player, he was consistency personified. He scored 248 goals in those 499 games for the Hammers, an average of almost exactly a goal every two games.

Geoff had almost been lost to cricket, having represented Essex in his youth but having signed for Ted Fenton at West Ham, blossomed under Ron Greenwood, and of course Sir Alf Ramsey. He scored 40 goals in total for West Ham in the year of England's World Cup success, and went one better a year later. Forever famed for his World Cup Final hat-trick, in October 1968 he scored six goals in 53 blistering minutes as Sunderland's record defeat was equalled at the Boleyn Ground. An FA Cup and European Cup Winners' Cup winner with West Ham, Hurst later played for Stoke, WBA, Seattle Sounders and Cork Celtic, coached England and managed Chelsea.

JIM **BARRETT** 467 **PLUS 86 WAR-TIME GAMES**

War-time games don't count in official records, but an honourable mention nonetheless for Jim Barnett who played 467 times in the 15 years leading up to World War Two, and added another 86 in war-time matches.

Jim first played at the Boleyn Ground in 1920/21 for West Ham Boys against Liverpool Boys in an English Schools game. In October 1928 he was picked to play for England against Northern Ireland but was injured after only four minutes. Nonetheless, in the game played at Goodison Park, England still won 2-1 with a winner from Everton's Dixie Dean. Jim's son, James, played 87 games for the Hammers from 1949 to 1955.

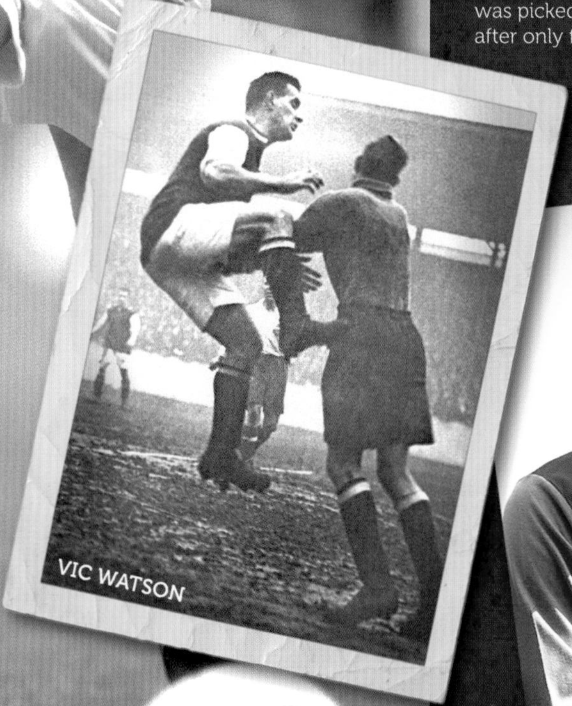

VIC WATSON

GEOFF HURST

JIM BARRETT

55

BOBBY **MOORE** OBE 546

Probably the finest defender to ever play for England and definitely the only man to ever captain England to a World Cup win! Images of Bobby with the Jules Rimet trophy at Wembley in 1966, or his tackle and subsequent final whistle greeting with Pelé at the 1970 World Cup are embedded indelibly in the memories of every supporter old enough to have seen him play. Born in 1941, Bobby passed away far too early in 1993.

From 6 October 1956 when he made his first appearance for West Ham Colts to 9 March 1974 when he wore the Claret and Blue for the last time in a reserve game with Plymouth Argyle, Bobby was at the heart of the Club. To many, he still is. A first-team debut in September 1958 was followed by a first game as captain in April 1962, a month before his England debut. Within a year he was captain of his country and a further year on, Footballer of the Year and captain of the FA Cup winners. The European Cup Winners' Cup came along in 1965 but of course it was in the 1966 World Cup he reached his peak.

He would have a testimonial against Celtic in 1970, win his 100th cap against Scotland in February 1972 and beat Jimmy Ruffell's tally as West Ham's highest appearance maker 12 months later. Five days after that last game for the Hammers second string he signed for Fulham with whom he would play against West Ham in the FA Cup Final of 1975.

There were later spells playing in the USA and managing Oxford City and Southend United but the four-time Hammer of the Year; who ended with 108 England caps, 90 of them as captain, will always be remembered as the man who raised glittering trophies at Wembley for three successive seasons, the last of them proclaiming England as Champions of the World.

ALL COMPETITIONS, INCLUDING MINOR ONES, ARE INCLUDED IN THE APPEARANCE TOTALS.

THE 600 CLUB

FRANK **LAMPARD** (Senior) 674

A massively dependable left back who was a stalwart of the Club from his debut against Manchester City in November 1967 to his departure in 1985, when he moved on to finish his playing days with Southend United under the management of his old team-mate Bobby Moore.

Frank won the FA Cup with West Ham in 1975 and 1980 as well as winning promotion in 1981. He won the first of his two full England caps against Yugoslavia in October 1982 and is the father of Frank Lampard Junior.

SIR TREVOR **BROOKING** 647

Sir Trevor has just left his job as the FA's Director of Football Development in 2014. It is a post he held since 2003 and there is no one better placed to advance the cause of skilful and thoughtful football than the man who bestrode the Boleyn Ground as a midfield maestro from his debut in 1967 until 1984.

An FA Cup winner in 1975 and 1980, he scored the winner against Arsenal in the latter final, with a rare header. Capped 47 times by England, for whom he scored five times, he had two successful spells in charge of the West Ham team in 2003 and now has the stand to the left of the players' tunnel named the Sir Trevor Brooking Stand.

ALVIN **MARTIN** 600

Big Alvin Martin continued in the fine tradition of excellent, and often elegant defenders at West Ham. A Merseysider, born 41 days before Bobby Moore made his West Ham debut, Alvin spent two decades at the Boleyn Ground, commencing a couple of years after Bobby Moore had left the Club.

An FA Cup winner in 1975, Martin had the distinction of not only scoring a hat-trick for West Ham as a defender but doing so with a goal against three different goalkeepers in an 8-1 thumping of Newcastle United in April 1986. His own son David went on to become a goalkeeper while another son Joe continued in the family tradition as a defender.

First capped by Ron Greenwood against Brazil in 1981, Alvin was ruled out of the 1982 World Cup by injury but played in the 1986 tournament. In total he played 17 times for England while at West Ham. His value was illustrated by the fact that he shared with Billy Bonds the distinction of having two testimonials - against Spurs in 1988 and Chelsea seven years later. After leaving the club Martin had a season with Leyton Orient and two as manager of Southend.

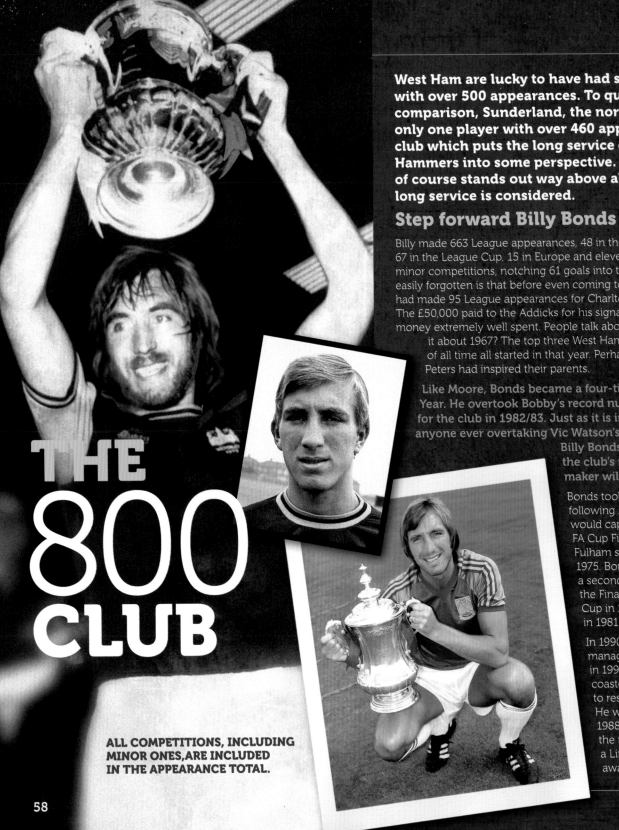

West Ham are lucky to have had so many servants with over 500 appearances. To quote one random comparison, Sunderland, the north east club have only one player with over 460 appearances for the club which puts the long service of so many Hammers into some perspective. One man of course stands out way above all others when long service is considered.

Step forward Billy Bonds MBE.

Billy made 663 League appearances, 48 in the FA Cup, an amazing 67 in the League Cup, 15 in Europe and eleven others in assorted minor competitions, notching 61 goals into the bargain. What is easily forgotten is that before even coming to West Ham, Bonds had made 95 League appearances for Charlton Athletic as well. The £50,000 paid to the Addicks for his signature in May 1967 was money extremely well spent. People talk about 1966, but what was it about 1967? The top three West Ham appearance makers of all time all started in that year. Perhaps Moore, Hurst and Peters had inspired their parents.

Like Moore, Bonds became a four-time Hammer of the Year. He overtook Bobby's record number of appearances for the club in 1982/83. Just as it is impossible to imagine anyone ever overtaking Vic Watson's goals tally, surely Billy Bonds' place in history as the club's record appearance maker will never be beaten.

Bonds took over as captain following Moore's departure and would captain West Ham in the FA Cup Final victory over a Fulham side including Bobby in 1975. Bonds would win the Cup a second time in 1980 and reach the Finals of the Cup Winners' Cup in 1976 and League Cup in 1981.

In 1990 Billy became West Ham manager, winning promotion in 1991 and 1993 in a roller coaster era before he decided to resign in August 1994. He was awarded the MBE in 1988 and in 2013 he became the first person to receive a Lifetime Achievement award from West Ham.

THE 800 CLUB

ALL COMPETITIONS, INCLUDING MINOR ONES, ARE INCLUDED IN THE APPEARANCE TOTAL.

BILLY
BONDS
MBE
804

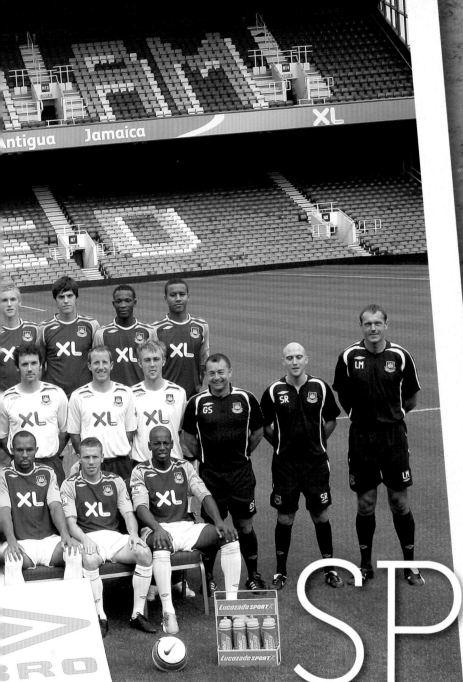

Which year do you think this picture was taken?

You'll find the answer on page 82, but see if you can work it out.

Ever-presents Robert Green and George McCartney were the Hammer of the Year and runner-up.

Only two other players, Hayden Mullins and Lucas Neill managed over 30 starts with the lack of a settled side one reason why Alan Curbishley's side had to settle for tenth place in the Barclays Premier League.

Dean Ashton top scored with ten league goals but no one else managed more than four. The best win of the season was a 5-0 victory at Derby with the other side of the coin being a dreadful start to March which saw three consecutive 4-0 defeats. There was a decent run to the quarter-final in what was then the Carling Cup.

SPOT THE SEASON

BACK ROW: (left to right) Kieran Sadlier, Amos Nasha, Sam Westley, Tim Brown, Sam Howes, Taylor Tombides, Jaanai Gordon, Matthias Fanimo.
MIDDLE ROW: (left to right) Josh Pask, Reece Oxford, Kieran Bywater, Moses Makasi, Sebastian Lletget, Blair Turgott, Dan Potts, Nathan Mavila.
FRONT ROW: (left to right) Elliot Lee, Lewis Page, Lee Harrison (Head Academy Goalkeeping Coach), Tom Smith (Head of Sports Science & Medicine), Nick Haycock (Professional Development Phase Lead Coach), Greg De Carnys (Head of Performance), Ben Marlow, Josh Cullen.

The Development Squad

For decades, West Ham United have been synonymous with the discovery and development of the best young footballers in the country.

On their graduation from the Academy of Football at the age of 18, young professionals and third-year scholars move into the Development Squad.

Overseen by Academy Manager and Head of Coaching and Player Development Terry Westley and managed by Nick Haycock, West Ham's Development Squad compete in the Barclays U21 Premier League Division One.

Kieran **Bywater**

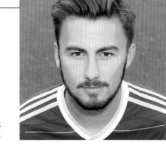

BORN: 7 September 1995,
Trafford, Manchester, England

POSITION: Attacking midfielder

Kieran is a free-scoring attacking
midfielder who topped the goal charts
for West Ham United's U18s in 2013/14
with 17 in 30 appearances.

He captained the youth team to the Barclays U18 Premier League
Play-Off semi-finals in spring 2014, where they were edged out by
Manchester City. He totalled seven Development Squad appearances in
2013/14 and signed his first professional contract with West Ham United
in the summer. He was also nominated for the Dylan Tombides Award
for the Club's Outstanding Academy Scholar for 2013/14.

Leo **Chambers**

BORN: 5 August 1995,
London, England

POSITION: Defender

Leo, who joined the Academy in 2002
when he was just seven-years-old, is
able to play at right back or centre
back.

He progressed through the Academy
ranks to sign his first professional contract at the age of 17 in 2012 and
made his first-team debut for West Ham United in a 2-1 League Cup
second-round victory over Cheltenham Town at the Boleyn Ground on
27 August 2013.

He wore the captain's armband on his England U16 debut in a Victory
Shield international against Wales in October 2010 and has been capped
by England at U16, U17, U18 and U19 levels.

Josh **Cullen**

BORN: 7 April 1996,
Southend-on-Sea, England

POSITION: Midfielder

An all-action central midfielder
who has made 43 League and Cup
appearances for the U18s over two
seasons between 2012 and 2014.

Last season Josh played ten U21
games and won the Dylan Tombides Award for being the Academy's
Outstanding Scholar for the 2013/14 season.

Capped by England at U16 level before switching his allegiance to the
Republic of Ireland in early 2014, he made his Ireland debut at U18 level
in a friendly against Czech Republic in April 2014.

Matthias **Fanimo**

BORN: 28 January 1994,
Lambeth, London, England

POSITION: Winger

Matthias was spotted by West Ham
United at the age of six while playing
for Redriff Primary School. He signed
his first professional contract with the
Club in the summer of 2011 and made
his first-team debut for the Hammers as a substitute in a League Cup
second-round win over Cheltenham Town at the Boleyn Ground on
28 August 2012. He appeared again as a substitute in the League Cup
third round defeat by Wigan Athletic in September 2012 and made his
third first-team appearance for West Ham United as a substitute in a 5-0
FA Cup third-round defeat at Nottingham Forest in January 2014. He
was loaned to League Two club Hartlepool United in September 2014.

He has been capped by England at U16, U17 and U18 levels. He won the
Victory Shield home international tournament with England U16s in
2008 and captained his country in the 2009 Victory Shield.

Jaanai **Gordon**

BORN: 7 December 1995,
Northampton, England

POSITION: Forward

Gordon came through the Academy
ranks at Peterborough United, signing
his first professional contract with the
Posh on his 17th birthday in 2012.

He made seven first-team appearances
for Peterborough before trialling with
West Ham United in autumn 2013. He scored twice in the opening game
of his U18 trial against Aston Villa and joined the Hammers on New
Year's Day 2014. He was an unused substitute for the FA Cup third-round
defeat at Nottingham Forest in January 2014.

Jamie **Harney**

BORN: 4 March 1996, Plumbridge,
County Tyrone, Northern Ireland

POSITION: Defender

Northern Irish centre back Jamie who
joined West Ham United in 2012 as a
first-year scholar at the age of 16. He
made 17 appearances and netted twice
for the U18s in his first season with the
Club in 2012/13 and made his U21
debut as a substitute at Norwich City on
17 October 2012.

Jamie's been capped for Northern Ireland at all age-group levels
and captained his Country to glory in the U19 Milk Cup in August 2014.
His first Northern Ireland U21 start came in a 4-1 UEFA European U21
Championship qualifier in Serbia on 9 September 2014.

Dymon **Labonne**

BORN: 22 November 1994, Redbridge, London, England

POSITION: Winger

Dymon joined West Ham United at the age of 12 having previously played Sunday League football. He signed a two-year scholarship with West Ham United in summer 2011 and featured for the U18s at the Tallinn Cup pre-season tournament in Estonia in summer 2011. He suffered a serious knee injury in training in September 2011 which restricted him to just one substitute appearance for the U18s in 2012/13 and he did not make a competitive appearance in 2013/14. He was granted an extension to his scholarship in summer 2014 before returning to action in a pre-season win at Braintree Town in July 2014 and also appeared as a substitute in a 5-1 friendly win over an Ipswich Town XI in September 2014.

Elliot **Lee**

BORN: 16 December 1994, Durham, England

POSITION: Forward

Stocky and powerful, the striker is blessed with a natural finisher's ability and has been prolific at all age-group levels for the Hammers. The son of former West Ham United and England midfielder Rob Lee, he made his senior debut for the Hammers in an FA Cup third-round defeat at Manchester United in January 2013. Elliot made his Barclays Premier League bow for West Ham United in the home defeat by Stoke City on 31 August 2013 before going out on loan to Colchester United in October 2013, making four League One appearances and scoring his maiden Football League goal at Rotherham United on 2 November 2013.

Sebastian **Lletget**

BORN: 3 September 1992, San Francisco, California, United States

POSITION: Attacking midfielder

California-born, United States U23 international Sebastian is an attacking midfielder blessed with outstanding technical ability. He was the first product of the West Ham United International Academy to sign professional terms, doing so in September 2010. He scored three goals in 19 appearances for the Development Squad in 2013/14 and made his first-team debut for the Hammers in the FA Cup third-round defeat at Nottingham Forest in January 2014. He also featured in the first-team pre-season matches at Ipswich Town and Schalke 04 in July 2014. Sebastian has been capped by United States at U15, U17, U20 and U23 levels.

Sean **Maguire**

BORN: 1 May 1994, Luton, England

POSITION: Forward

The Bedfordshire-born Republic of Ireland U19 striker joined West Ham United in January 2013 following a prolific spell with League of Ireland First Division side Waterford United where he netted 14 goals in 32 appearances to attract the attention of West Ham United.

He was an unused substitute in the FA Cup third-round defeat at Nottingham Forest in January 2014 before going out on loan to League of Ireland Premier Division side Sligo Rovers in the spring, making more than 20 first-team appearances for the club and playing twice in the UEFA Europa League against Norwegian club Rosenborg.

In September he moved on loan to League Two club Accrington Stanley and scored on his debut in a 5-4 win at Northampton Town.

Moses **Makasi**

BORN: 22 September 1995, London, England

POSITION: Midfielder

A defensive midfielder who is strong in the tackle and composed in possession.

He was a regular for the U18s in the second year of his scholarship in 2013/14, making 28 appearances and starting the Development Squad's final eight league matches of the season.

Moses agreed his first professional deal with West Ham United in summer 2014.

Ben **Marlow**

BORN: 1 October 1995, Chelmsford, England

POSITION: Midfielder

A tough-tackling Essex-born central midfielder who joined West Ham United at the age of six.

An injury-restricted 2013/14 season saw him make just nine U18 appearances, scoring one goal. In the summer, Ben had his scholarship extended to a third season.

Nathan **Mavila**

BORN: 15 October 1995,
Brixton, London, England

POSITION: Full back/Winger

Nathan who joined West Ham United from Wycombe Wanderers at the age of 16 in summer 2012 is happy to play full back or winger.

Born and raised in London to Congolese parents the speedy, direct player is never afraid to deliver a telling cross or shot. He scored on his Development Squad debut in a 3-1 league defeat at Norwich City in December 2012. Last season he totalled nine Barclays U21 Premier League appearances, scoring one goal and was also a semi-regular for the U18s appearing on 29 occasions.

Paul **McCallum**

BORN: 28 July 1993,
Streatham, London, England

POSITION: Forward

Tall and powerful, Paul joined West Ham United in January 2011 following a prolific spell with non-league Dulwich Hamlet. He scored 15 goals in just seven appearances in the FA Youth Cup in 2010/11, helping Dulwich Hamlet to reach the third round before having spells with League Two outfits Rochdale and AFC Wimbledon.

He signed a new Hammers contract in January 2013 and appeared in first-team pre-season matches at Cork City, where he scored, Borehamwood and AFC Bournemouth in July 2013 before being loaned out again to Torquay United and Scottish Premier League club Heart of Midlothian.

Amos **Nasha**

BORN: 4 September 1995,
Finchley, London, England

POSITION: Defender

Amos is a versatile player able to perform at full back, centre back or in a defensive midfield role. He began his career with the Lyndhurst Boys club in Islington and joined the Hammers at the age of 12 after being released by Spurs.

He appeared for the Hammers' U18s while still a schoolboy in 2011/12 and as a substitute in the first-team pre-season matches at Southend United and Oxford United in summer 2012 at the age of 16. Last term he totalled five U21 appearances and made 26 starts for the U18s, scoring twice.

Lewis Page

BORN: 20 May 1996, London, England

POSITION: Defender

The attack-minded left back made 19 appearances for the U18s in 2012/13 as a first-year scholar, 18 of them starts, and appeared for the Development Squad on five occasions during the second year of his scholarship in 2013/14. After being nominated for the Dylan Tombides Academy Player of the Year for 2013/14 Lewis signed his first professional contract in summer 2014.

Dan **Potts**

BORN: 13 April 1994,
Barking, London, England

POSITION: Defender

A versatile and composed defender Dan is able to play at centre back or left back. He followed his famous father Steve through the ranks at the Academy of Football, captaining the U18s and U21s regularly and was rewarded with a first professional contract and first-team debut in the same week in December 2011. Made his debut in the 1-0 Championship win over Barnsley at the Boleyn Ground making four first-team appearances in total that season. After loan spells with Colchester United and Portsmouth he signed a new contract with West Ham United in the summer of 2014. Was capped by the United States at U20 level before switching his allegiance to England in 2012 and has played for England at U18, U19 and U20 level.

Kieran **Sadlier**

BORN: 14 September 1994,
Haywards Heath, England

POSITION: Forward

The Republic of Ireland U21 international was initially scouted by Cambridge United as an under-nine before joining West Ham United when Cambridge United's own Academy closed in 2005. He progressed through the ranks before a shin injury in November 2013 slowed his development. Kieran returned to action in February 2014 and ended the season with 15 U21 appearances and three goals to his name before spending the summer working with Olympic sprint champion Michael Johnson at St George's Park. Capped by the Republic of Ireland at U18 and U19 levels, he made his U21 debut against Qatar U23s in Aachen, Germany, on 24 May 2014.

Taylor **Tombides**

BORN: 21 February 1996,
Perth, Western Australia, Australia

POSITION: Attacking midfielder/Forward

Australia-born Taylor can play both in attacking midfield or in the forward line. His appearances were limited by a serious injury in 2013/14, meaning he played just once for the U18s. Taylor is the younger brother of Dylan Tombides, the striker who tragically passed away earlier this year at the age of 20 following a three-year battle with cancer. He dedicated his goal in the Development Squad's pre-season victory over AFC Hornchurch in July 2014 to his older brother. He has been capped by Australia at U16 level and scored five goals as a substitute for Australia U16s in a 10-0 AFC U16 Championship qualifying win over Guam in Thailand in September 2011.

Blair **Turgott**

BORN: 22 May 1994,
Bromley, Kent, England

POSITION: Winger

Blair joined the Hammers at the age of eight. He has enjoyed a series of loan spells in the Football League in recent seasons, most notably helping Bradford City reach the Capital One Cup Final in 2012/13 and appearing in the quarter-final and semi-final wins over Barclays Premier League Arsenal and Aston Villa respectively.

He made his Hammers debut in the FA Cup third-round defeat at Nottingham Forest in January 2014 before being loaned out again to Rotherham United the same month. He had a further loan spell with League Two club Dagenham and Redbridge.

He played alongside Liverpool's Raheem Sterling for England U17s as they defeated Argentina on penalties before being edged out 3-2 by Germany in the 2011 FIFA U17 World Cup quarter-finals. He has been capped by England at U16, U17, U18 and U19 levels, scoring three goals in six games for the U19s.

Sam **Westley**

BORN: 4 February 1994, England

POSITION: Full back

Sam is a defender who is happy to play in either full back position. He was with Birmingham City as a schoolboy and scholar before joining Stoke City at the age of 18 in summer 2012. After two seasons with Stoke City's Development Squad, he spent some time with Ipswich Town in the spring of 2014 before joining West Ham United in the summer. He made his Hammers debut in a Barclays U21 Premier League defeat at Tottenham Hotspur on 18 August 2014.

Danny **Whitehead**

BORN: 23 October 1993,
Stretford, Manchester, England

POSITION: Midfielder

Danny began his career with Stockport County at the age of 14 in 2008 and penned a two-year deal when he signed for West Ham United from the Conference North club in summer 2013. A first-team player at Stockport County at just 17 he totalled 42 appearances for the Hatters in 2012/13.

Last term he made 21 appearances, scoring two goals, for the Development Squad and he made his Hammers debut in an FA Cup third-round defeat at Nottingham Forest in January 2014. At the beginning of this season Danny appeared in the first-team pre-season matches against Stevenage, Wellington Phoenix and Sydney FC.

Under-18s

The U18s headed into 2014/15 on the back of a fine season in the Barclays U18 Premier League, having finished second in the South Division last year. Steve Potts and his squad will be on the hunt for more success this time around.

Fatai **Adebayo**

BORN: 11 September 1997

POSITION: Forward

17-year-old forward Fatai Adebayo is a local lad, hailing from Canning Town. He joined the Club at U13 level so is now in his fifth year with the Hammers. An attacking midfielder who is also capable of playing further forward, he possesses a deadly left foot. Adebayo has made his Under-18s bow this season as he embarks on his Hammers scholarship.

Jeremiah **Amoo**

BORN: 10 June 1997

POSITION: Forward

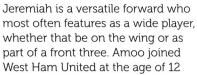

Jeremiah is a versatile forward who most often features as a wide player, whether that be on the wing or as part of a front three. Amoo joined West Ham United at the age of 12 and made his U18s breakthrough last season, scoring twice in 17 games at that level. He was also used by Nick Haycock for the Development Squad and found the net once in only two games.

Olatunji **Akinola**

BORN: 21 November 1998

POSITION: Centre back

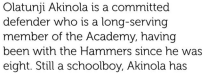

Olatunji Akinola is a committed defender who is a long-serving member of the Academy, having been with the Hammers since he was eight. Still a schoolboy, Akinola has been a regular for the U16s side for the last couple of seasons. He made two Under-18s appearances last season, before he has even reached his 16th birthday and will be hopeful of more opportunities at that level this term.

Kieran **Bailey**

BORN: 25 December 1996

POSITION: Attacking midfielder

Attacking midfielder Kieran Bailey is a player who loves to create chances for his fellow teammates. The second year scholar joined the Academy when he was eight-years-old, meaning he has now been with the Club for nearly a decade.

Bailey possesses two good feet and he made good progress in the first year of his scholarship, with seven Under-18s appearances to his name. Featuring regularly in the opening weeks of this campaign, he will hope to build on that number in the months ahead.

Clarke **Bogard**

BORN: 29 October 1997

POSITION: Goalkeeper

Clarke Bogard is one of the longest serving players in the West Ham Academy, having joined the Club at just seven-years-old. Now 17, he has been with the Hammers for ten years, progressing onto his scholarship.

Now he will be looking to kick-on during his first full year with the Under-18 squad. Having played regularly for the Under-16s and older age groups, he has already featured with the Under-21s too and looks set for a bright future.

Dan **Boness**

BORN: 7 November 1997

POSITION: Goalkeeper

The latest goalkeeper to join the Academy is Dan Boness, who was recruited from Ipswich Town in the summer of 2014.

Now a first year scholar, he is highly-regarded. Despite only being with the Hammers for a short period of time, he has already settled in at the Club, appearing for Nick Haycock's Development Squad in pre-season and taking his place on the bench for the U21s' league clash with Sunderland at the Boleyn Ground in September.

Oscar **Borg**

BORN: 5 September 1997
POSITION: Left back

Left-sided player Oscar Borg joined West Ham United's Academy as an Under-13. The 17-year-old is now a first year scholar and his eye-catching performances at age-group level caught the eye of several suitors last season, but he committed his future to the Club earlier this year.

A regular in the Under-16s last season, Oscar also stepped up to make three Under-18s appearances. Now a full-time member of the Under-18s squad, Oscar will look to maintain his fine progress in 2014/15.

Tim **Brown**

BORN: 12 June 1997
POSITION: Goalkeeper

Second-year scholar Tim Brown has been with the Academy since joining as an Under-16 two summers ago. Despite his tender years, he has already gained first team experience at non-league level, having been loaned to Isthmian League Premier Division side Dulwich Hamlet last year.

He is currently enjoying a similar spell at Canvey Island in the same division, and has played above his age group with the Hammers, appearing twice at Under-21 level in 2013/14.

Jordan **Brown**

BORN: 10 November 1996
POSITION: Striker

Jordan Brown is a second year scholar with the West Ham United Academy, who has made a terrific impact since joining the Club from Arsenal in 2013. Having played for England at age-group level, he netted 12 goals in 26 matches for the Under-18s last term, as well as notching three goals in seven Under-21 games. Brown's red hot goalscoring form continued at the start of 2014/15, with six goals from his opening seven matches.

Marcus **Browne**

BORN: 18 December 1997
POSITION: Midfielder

Marcus Browne is another player who has been with the Academy since the age of eight. He was absent with injury for a large part of the 2013/14 campaign, but has returned to make a good start to this campaign - his first as a scholar.

Browne is a serious threat from dead ball situations and scored an incredible free-kick in a game against Real Madrid last year. He will hope to add to his burgeoning reputation with similar strikes this term.

Reece **Burke**

BORN: 2 September 1996
POSITION: Centre back

Accomplished defender Reece Burke will already be well known to West Ham United fans having made the step up to the first team squad on several occasions already. The second-year scholar made eight U21s appearances last term despite his young age and even debuted for the first team in the FA Cup at Nottingham Forest.

Having recently signed his first professional contract, he started a senior game for the first time this season when the Hammers took on Sheffield United in the Capital One Cup.

Grady **Diangana**

BORN: 19 April 1998
POSITION: Attacking midfielder

Grady Diangana is an attacking midfielder with plenty of flair, unsurprising for someone who claims Ronaldinho as an influence on his play. He linked up with West Ham United at the age of 12 and was originally a striker. He was converted to a midfielder when he was playing for the Under-15s and is another prospect who has already featured for the Under-21s. He played five Under-18s games last season and has started 2014/15 in fine fashion.

Ross **Elsom**

BORN: 22 December 1997

POSITION: Midfield

Ross Elsom is a first year scholar who will be looking to kick-on with the Under-18s in 2014/15. He joined the Club from non-league Billericay Town, responding well to the step up with the West Ham United Academy. After a string of impressive performances for the Under-16 side, he moved into the Under-18s late in the 2013/14 campaign and will target more run-outs as he sets out on his scholarship at Little Heath.

Jahmal **Hector-Ingram**

BORN: 11 November 1998

POSITION: Winger/Forward

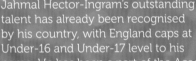

Jahmal Hector-Ingram's outstanding talent has already been recognised by his country, with England caps at Under-16 and Under-17 level to his name. He has been a part of the Academy since the age of eight, impressing in every age group in which he has played.

A goalscorer who can play out wide or at the point of the attack, Hector-Ingram notched for the Under-18s for this first time at the start of this season and will target many more goals this term.

Sam **Howes**

BORN: 10 November 1997

POSITION: Goalkeeper

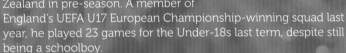

First year scholar Sam Howes has already made a name for himself with the Hammers, forming part of the first team squad which jetted out to New Zealand in pre-season. A member of England's UEFA U17 European Championship-winning squad last year, he played 23 games for the Under-18s last term, despite still being a schoolboy.

The commanding goalkeeper joined West Ham from Crystal Palace when he was an Under-10 and his impressive form saw him named the Young Hammer of the Year for 2013/14.

Kyle **Knoyle**

BORN: 24 September 1996

POSITION: Right back

A relatively recent arrival on the Hammers Academy scene, having joined at the age of 13, right back Kyle was recommended to the Club by coaches at a Junior Hammers coaching event.

He has taken the step up to Academy football in his stride and made 20 Under-18s and eight Under-21s appearances in the 2013/14 campaign.

He has again featured regularly for the Under-21s this term in the second year of his scholarship and has represented England at age group level.

Joe **Linley**

BORN: 19 September 1997

POSITION: Right back

Seventeen-year-old right back Joe Linley has been with West Ham United since making the move to E13 from Colchester United at the age of ten.

Now an accomplished full back, Linley was originally a central midfielder when he came to the Club. However, he converted to a defender two years into his time with West Ham and has progressed impressively to his scholarship since, becoming a regular member of the Under-18s squad.

Vashon **Neufville**

BORN: 18 July 1999

POSITION: Left back

Left back Vashon Neufville is one of the youngest members of the Under-18s squad, recently moving up from the Under-16s even though he is still only 15 years of age. He was released by Chelsea at 13, but has found his feet with the Hammers.

A skilful defender, Neufville is already an England international and has become a regular in Steve Potts' squad for the Barclays U18 Premier League campaign this term.

Manny Onariase

BORN: 21 October 1996
POSITION: Centre back

Manny Onariase is a powerful defender who has been at West Ham United since the age of 12. Possessing bags of natural talent, Onariase is always a threat from set plays and he scored twice in the opening three games of this campaign. He rarely missed a game for Steve Potts' team last year, featuring on 22 occasions for the Under-18s, as well as twice for the Under-21s, he is again knocking on Nick Haycock's door as he looks to step up.

Reece Oxford

BORN: 16 December 1998
POSITION: Centre back

One of the jewels in the Academy's crown, 15-year-old defender Reece Oxford is already playing two age groups ahead of himself having become an Under-21s regular this season. He became a Hammer at U13 level and has captained England at U17s. His rapid rise through the youth ranks at Little Heath has not gone unnoticed, and he featured on the first team's bench for the Capital One Cup tie against Sheffield Utd in August.

Djair Parfitt-Williams

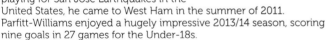

BORN: 10 January 1996
POSITION: Attacking midfielder

Bermuda-born attacker Djair Parfitt-Williams can play either as a striker, a No10 or out on either wing. His versatility makes him a threat all over the pitch and he has made great strides in recent years. Spotted by Hammers legend Clyde Best when he was playing for San Jose Earthquakes in the United States, he came to West Ham in the summer of 2011. Parfitt-Williams enjoyed a hugely impressive 2013/14 season, scoring nine goals in 27 games for the Under-18s.

Josh Pask

BORN: 1 November 1997
POSITION: Centre back

When Josh Pask joined the Academy aged just eight, his focus was on scoring goals rather than stopping them. Then a striker, he is now a very promising centre back who can also play as a holding midfielder. Pask put pen-to-paper on a two-year scholarship in the summer of 2014, having made nine appearances for the Under-18s last term. Josh played his first Barclays U21 Premier League game this season as he continues to impress.

Alex Pike

BORN: 8 February 1997
POSITION: Right back

Alex Pike arrived at the Academy when he was an Under-11s player, originally featuring in midfield. A local lad who played his formative football for Buckhurst Hill, Pike has become a very promising right back since first featuring in the position last season. The move saw him become a mainstay in the Hammers backline following an injury-disrupted first half of the campaign and he has continued in the same vein this season.

Joe Powell

BORN: 30 October 1998
POSITION: Central midfielder

Another young member of the Academy squad, Joe Powell is now in the final year of schoolboy football and will be pushing towards the Under-18s over the coming months. He predominately features at Under-16s, but is knocking on the door for a call-up and does already possess Under-18s experience. He joined West Ham United as an eight-year-old and is a hard-working holding midfielder, looking to follow in the footsteps of the many fine players who have come through the Academy.

Decarrey Sheriff

BORN: 18 February 1998
POSITION: Left wing/forward

Predominately a left winger, Decarrey Sheriff is a relative newcomer on the Hammers scene, signing up as a 14-year-old. He underwent trials at Arsenal before deciding to join the Hammers and has since progressed to become a first-year scholar. Currently going through the transition between Under-16 and Under-18 football, Sheriff looks to have a bright future in the game.

Noha Sylvestre

BORN: 29 December 1997
POSITION: Central midfielder

Noha left his native Switzerland to sign for West Ham United a year-and-a-half ago. He immediately settled into the Under-16s squad upon his arrival, prior to commencing his scholarship in the summer of 2014. Thriving with the step-up, the combative holding midfielder was a fixture in Steve Potts' squad over pre-season and has continued along the same path at the start of the Barclays U18 Premier League campaign.

THE LADIES

Jess **Barling**

POSITION: Defender

Left-back Jess is now in her second spell with the Club having previously spent a number of seasons with the Hammers before departing in summer 2013. She was part of the Ladies squad which won the Essex FA County Cup in 2009, defeating Colchester United 9-0 in the final. Jess made 21 appearances in all competitions in 2012/13 and returned to West Ham near the end of pre-season this summer.

Ruby **Baxter**

POSITION: Defender

Ruby is a centre back who rejoined the Ladies from Bristol Academy in summer 2014 after featuring for the club at U12 level. She appeared for Leyton Orient's Centre of Excellence when The FA introduced a one-club rule as a schoolgirl, preventing her from continuing to play for both clubs. Strong both in the air and on the floor Ruby started every one of the Ladies' pre-season fixtures this summer and made her competitive senior debut for the Ladies in a 2-1 league win at QPR on 24 August 2014.

Kelley **Blanchflower**

POSITION: Midfielder

Kelley is an attacking midfielder who joined the Hammers at the start of 2011/12, having formerly played for Arsenal Ladies Academy. She started her West Ham career positively but in September 2012 suffered a major injury setback when she fell awkwardly during a league game at QPR and broke her collarbone. Last season Kelley netted nine goals in 22 games in all competitions to finish as the Club's top scorer. She scored the Ladies' second goal in their Essex FA County Cup final win over Barking in April and scored the winner in the opening day League win at QPR on 24 August 2014.

Katie **Bottom**

POSITION: Defender/Midfielder

Katie, a lifelong Hammers fan who works for West Ham United Community Sports Trust as a coach, initially joined West Ham United Juniors at the age of twelve. She soon established herself in the Academy side that dominated girls' football at that level. She played 15 times in all competitions in 2012/13, scoring once and last season she totalled 18 appearances and one goal. She started her career as a midfielder before moving to left-back in 2013/14.

April **Bowers**

POSITION: Midfielder

April, who can play as an attacking midfielder, winger or forward, joined the Ladies at the age of 15 and progressed through the Club's junior teams before breaking into the first-team squad in 2011/12, where she scored twice in 18 games. She found the net four times in the 13-2 Essex FA County Cup win over Witham Town in February 2013, totalling seven goals in 20 appearances that season. She made eight appearances in 2013/14 including one as a substitute in the Essex FA County Cup Final win over Barking.

Alma **Donohoe**

POSITION: Midfielder

Alma, a quick and skilful attacking midfield player, joined West Ham United from Mile End-based KIKK United in summer 2014 after scoring seven goals for them in 2013/14. She studied for a BA and MA in Economics at the University of Cambridge and for a Masters in Business Administration at Harvard Business School, and away from football works in investment banking.

Vicky **King**

POSITION: Defender

Vicky is an experienced full-back and is the Ladies' longest-serving player, having initially joined West Ham United in 1998. She came on as a substitute in the 2011 Essex FA County Cup Final win over Hutton and in 2012/13 she made 23 appearances. Last season she played 22 games, scoring once and in April she started in the Essex FA County Cup Final win over Barking. In four pre-season fixtures she netted twice.

Vicky **Kinsman**

POSITION: Forward

Vicky was one of five players to join West Ham United in the summer. She played for the Hammers as a teenager then spent two seasons with Barking before giving up football to get married and start a family. She returned to Barking in summer 2013 and started their 5-1 Essex FA County Cup Final defeat by the Hammers in April 2014.

Zoe **Lipley-Hinton**

POSITION: Midfielder/Forward

Zoe joined West Ham United from Herongate Athletic Girls at the age of 15 and came through the U16 side and Development Squad before joining the first-team in 2012/13. She played 19 times in 2012/13, scoring once in the League Cup against Colchester United. Last season she netted once in 19 first-team games and also started the 2014 Essex FA County Cup Final victory.

Stacey **Little**

POSITION: Midfielder

Club and first-team captain Stacey is a goal-scoring midfielder and lifelong Hammers Fan. She played junior football for Hatfield Youth and began her career with QPR before spending three seasons with Charlton Athletic, then joining West Ham in summer 2010. In October 2013 she suffered a serious career threatening ankle injury. She was appointed captain in February 2014 and led the Hammers to Essex FA County Cup Final glory against Barking two months later.

Whitney **Locke**

POSITION: Forward

Whitney joined West Ham United from West Billericay Ladies in summer 2014 after training with the Club during the latter part of last season. She scored twice on her Development Squad debut in a 3-2 home league win over C&K Basildon on 7 September 2014.

Sarah **McCrea**

POSITION: Midfielder

Sarah, who joined West Ham from Charlton in December 2013, can play as an attacking midfielder or winger. She started her career with junior club Newlaithes in her home city of Carlisle and has also played for Blackburn Rovers and Preston North End. Sarah scored five goals in 12 games in her first half-season with the Hammers including finding the net in the 5-1 Essex FA County Cup Final victory over Barking in April 2014.

Lily **Mellors**

POSITION: Midfielder

Lily began her career with Colchester United as an Under-10 before joining West Ham United in November 2012. Last season she netted five times in 19 games in all competitions, including three in three Essex FA County Cup ties which included scoring the opener in the 5-1 Essex FA County Cup Final win over Barking in April.

Danica **Revell**

POSITION: Defender

Danica spent time with Leyton Orient's Centre of Excellence as a youngster before she joined West Ham United as a teenager in 2009. She graduated from the Club's junior sides into the first-team squad and started the 2012 Essex FA County Cup Final win over Hutton. In 2011/12 she was named Young Player of the Year but last season she only played 14 times, with a knee injury restricting her availability.

Nikita **Runnacles**

POSITION: Goalkeeper

Nikita joined the Ladies from Millwall Lionesses in summer 2014. She began her senior career with Colchester United Ladies, where she became No.1 goalkeeper and an assistant coach. She made her competitive debut for West Ham United in the 2-1 League win at Queens Park Rangers on 24 August 2014. Nikita is a full-time sports coach when not playing and also coaches the U15s at the Essex FA Centre of Excellence.

Emma **Sherwood**

POSITION: Forward

The skilful striker was the second of two players to join West Ham United from Millwall Lionesses in the summer. Emma began her career with Chelsea before joining Watford in summer 2011. She starred in pre-season finding the net five times, including a 'perfect' hat-trick at Denham Ladies and opened her competitive account for the Hammers in a League Cup first-round defeat at Keynsham Town on 31 August 2014.

West Ham finished 16th in the top flight when there was the unusual number of 21 clubs in the top division.

Tony Cottee (front row, third from right) was the only ever-present. He top-scored with 13 goals but was sold for a Club record £2m fee to Everton at the end of the season. Cottee's last goal was in the final home game when the biggest win of the season was achieved, Chelsea being thumped 4-1.

As one hero left another arrived. Not on the team picture but a debutant on 2 April at Sheffield Wednesday was Julian Dicks who would play the last eight games of the season.

In goal Tom McAlister (on the right of the three keepers) missed just one match. On that occasion he was replaced by Phil Parkes (to his right). Parkes was one of three men to play just once, the others being Neil Orr (middle row, second from left) and Alan Devonshire, (middle row, fifth from left). Hammer of the Year was Stewart Robson (middle row, fourth from right).

Can you spot the season?

Find the answer on page 82.

SPOT
THE SEASON

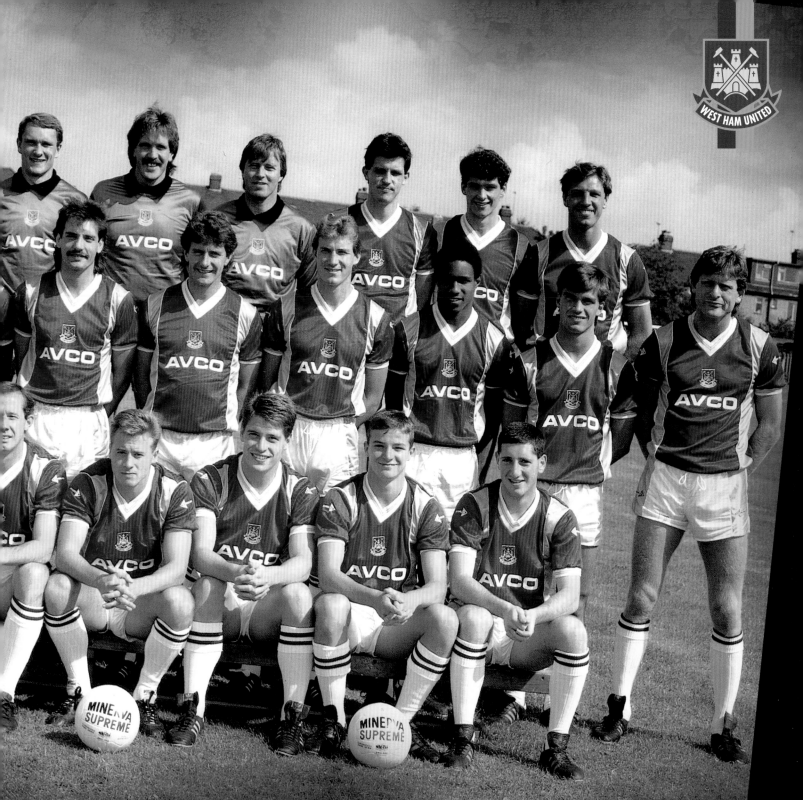

75

FAN-TASTIC

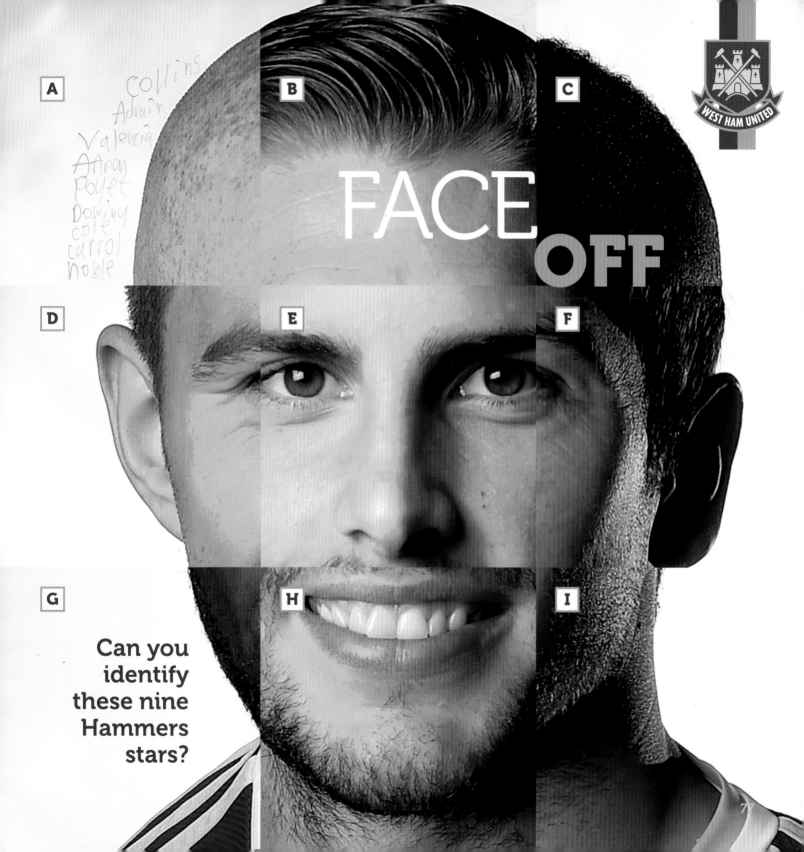

A

Collins
Adrain
Valencia
Aaron
Poyet
Dowing
cole
carrol
noble

B

C

FACE
OFF

D

E

F

G

H

I

Can you
identify
these nine
Hammers
stars?

WEST HAM UNITED

HAMMERABILIA

Many supporters like to collect Hammers items. Do you collect anything? Here we feature a small selection of items old and new (ish) that feature some of West Ham's biggest names - and one or two that aren't so well known.

TOMMY PEACE YEWS

Tommy was a right-winger signed for West Ham for £150 in 1924. Born in County Durham in 1902 he started his career with NER Athletic before moving on to Hartlepools (as they were known then), initially as an amateur in 1919. He became one of the Irons' early heroes, scoring 51 times in 361 games in all competitions as well as creating many more. A keen pianist, Tommy entertained his team-mates as well as the fans. He left West Ham in 1933, signing for Clapton Orient before becoming an engineer in the motor trade. Tommy died a month after seeing Bobby Moore lift the World Cup in 1966. He is pictured here on a John Player cigarette card featuring footballers of 1928/29.

ANOTHER CARD FROM THE 1928/29 JOHN PLAYER CIGARETTE CARD SERIES

This time of Stanley Earle who became a professional with West Ham. An amateur international when with Clapton Orient he had played for Arsenal before becoming a Hammer where he went on to become captain.

UNDOUBTEDLY WEST HAM'S MOST FAMOUS TRIO: THE MEN WHO WON THE WORLD CUP - BOBBY MOORE, GEOFF HURST AND MARTIN PETERS

Here their exploits in the 1966 World Cup Final are commemorated in drawings which show hat-trick hero Hurst with the Jules Rimet Trophy which the Queen had handed to skipper Bobby Moore. Martin Peters of course had underlined the West Ham stamp on England's win by scoring the other goal in the 4-2 victory over West Germany in the Final at Wembley.

THESE POSTCARDS WERE PRODUCED IN 1979 BY A COMPANY CALLED SIGMA SPORTS

They were part of a series of 60 given away with a book called The Supporters Football Form Book and Diary. The cover of this publication showed Kevin Keegan in an England kit while Alan Ball was card number one, George Best number four and Trevor Brooking the highest Hammer at number eight. Trevor is pictured here along with Bobby Moore and Geoff Hurst who were card numbers 46 and 32. A card (number 48) was also produced of Martin Peters.

PROBABLY THE MOST COMMON THING TO COLLECT IS PROGRAMMES

A ticket is a great souvenir of your attendance at a match but a programme gives you some context when looking back. Of course, for older supporters, they went to many a match where you just paid at the gate and did not have a ticket to keep and collect.

THE QUARTET OF PROGRAMME COVERS HERE ARE FROM WEST HAM'S FOUR WEMBLEY FA CUP FINALS: THE FIRST EVER WEMBLEY FINAL FROM 1923 AND THE WINS OF 1964, 1975 AND 1980.

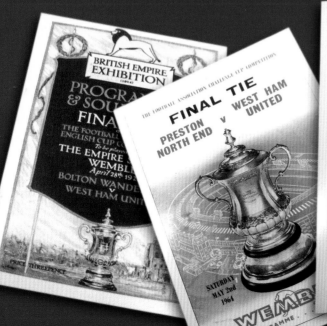

BILLY MOORE

GEORGE KAY

JIMMY RUFFELL

V. WATSON

TED HUFTON

WEST HAM U.

HAMMERABILIA

This season's official West Ham United programme is a hugely professional production full of good reading, not least the 'Hammerabilia' page compiled by collector Steve Marsh and a 'Get with the Programme' feature produced by Stuart Allen.

Match programmes are probably the best souvenir of a game. Having old tickets can be great too but a programme can tell the story. West Ham fans are fortunate to have had a high quality programme throughout the decades but away programmes can also shed light on the Hammers of the past.

The programme featured here is from a club at the other end of the country, Sunderland, but it has a special place in Hammers' history as it is from West Ham's first ever game in the top flight, back in 1923.

The modern 2014-15 programme of West Ham is a lavish 84 page, full colour, perfect bound publication. The programme for West Ham's visit to the north east on 25 August 1923 was a 20 page programme with a price of two old pence, the equivalent of a penny nowadays.

The cover of the programme was a generic cover for the season at Sunderland, featuring an advert for the local brewer, Vaux. West Ham, as the visiting side, did not merit a mention on the cover, only the date in the top left corner identifies it as the programme which heralds the Hammers' arrival at the top table of English football.

Once you turn the page, however, the expected teams of both West Ham and Sunderland are laid out, the Hammers' former Sunderland player Billy Moore is warmly welcomed back to Wearside, "The Southern air seems to have suited him but he was always a great little player," notes the programme. The game itself finished goalless and goodness knows how many of the 35,000 who attended the game bought a programme, which is still preserved now approaching a century later. What is certain is that a copy of this programme from West Ham's first ever top-flight fixture marks any Hammers collection as a top class one.

EAMS

Kick-off at 3.15

SUNDERLAND.

1
Robson

2
Cresswell

3
England

5
Parker

6
Poole

4
Wilkinson

10
Hawes

11
Ellis

7
Marshall

8
Buchan

9
Paterson

O

Ruffell
12

Moore
13

Watson
14

Brown
15

Richards
16

Tresadern
17

Kay
18

Bishop
19

Hodgson
20

Henderson
21

Hufton
22

WEST HAM

Referee :—Mr. H. W. Andrews.

Linesmen :—Messers, J. R. Thompson and W. Green.

SUNDERLAND
A.F.C.

Directors.
W. H. Bell. Esq.
(Chairman).
Walter Raine, Esq., J.P.
(Vice-Chairman).
Jos. M. Prior, Esq.
Geo. Short, Esq.

Directors—continued.
F. W. Taylor, Esq., J.P
E. W. Taylor, Esq.
Duncan White, Esq.
Samuel Wilson, Esq.

Secretary—R. H. Kyle.

NEWS and RECORD

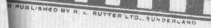

QUIZ ANSWERS

PAGE 24: SPOT THE SEASON
1974/75.

PAGE 26: 2014 QUIZ OF THE YEAR

1. Diafra Sakho. **2.** Hull City. **3.** Cardiff City.
4. The Marathonbet Cup. **5.** Reece Burke. **6.** Marco Borriello
and Antonio Nocerino. **7.** Stevenage. **8.** Mauro Zarate.
9. Kieran Bywater. **10.** Manchester United. **11.** FC Metz.
12. Carl Jenkinson. **13.** Morgan Amalfitano. **14.** Two against
Honduras and one against Switzerland. **15.** Five.
16. Swansea City, Aston Villa, Norwich City and Southampton.
17. Southampton who were defeated 3-1, the other three games
were all 2-0. **18.** Aaron Cresswell. **19.** Aaron Cresswell, Winston
Reid, Stewart Downing and Adrian. **20.** 19th.

PAGE 30: SPOT THE SEASON
1969/70.

PAGE 44: SPOT THE SEASON
1958/59.

PAGE 52: CUP FINALS QUIZ
1. 13 - 5 FA Cup finals, two legs of a League Cup final plus
another League Cup final and replay, two European Cup Winners'
Cup finals and two legs of an Intertoto Cup final.
2. John Sissons (1964 FA Cup final). **3.** Six (1923, 1964, 1965, 1975,
1980 and 1981). **4.** Two, the first legs of the 1966 League Cup
and 1999 Intertoto Cup finals. **5.** Alan Sealey (1965 ECWC) and
Alan Taylor (1975 FAC). **6.** Robbie Rensenbrink and Francois van
der Elst (1976 ECWC) and Steven Gerrard (2006 FAC).
7. Three (Ron Boyce 1964 FA Cup, Johnny Byrne 1966 League
Cup 1st leg and Ray Stewart, 1981 League Cup). **8.** Clemence.
Ray Clemence kept goal for Liverpool against the Hammers in
the 1981 League Cup final, all the others kept goal against West
Ham in FA Cup finals. **9.** Stuart Pearson. **10.** Two. **11.** No, it is
level with 21 goals scored for and against. **12.** It is level with five
triumphs and five defeats. **13.** Teddy Sheringham. **14.** Ticker.
15. Phil Parkes. **16.** Four (England, Wales, France & Belgium).
17. All three of Bobby Moore, Geoff Hurst and Martin Peters.
18. Trevor Booking. **19.** Pat Holland. **20.** Billy.

PAGE 60: SPOT THE SEASON
2007/08.

PAGE 74: SPOT THE SEASON
1987/88.

PAGE 76: FAN-TASTIC
Billy Bonds, Joe Cole, Paolo Di Canio, Bobby Moore
and Phil Parkes.

PAGE 77: FACE OFF
A. James Collins. **B.** Adrian. **C.** Enner Valencia.
D. Aaron Cresswell. **E.** Diego Poyet. **F.** Stewart Downing.
G. Carlton Cole. **H.** Andy Carroll. **I.** Mark Noble.